Psychology of the Japanese People

Psychology of the Japanese People

by Hiroshi Minami

Translated by
Albert R. Ikoma
under the auspices of the
East-West Center

UNIVERSITY OF TORONTO PRESS

Originally published in Japanese as *Nihonjin no shinri* by Iwanami Shoten, Tokyo, 1953

First published in Canada, the United States,
and other countries in the Americas by
University of Toronto Press, Toronto and
Buffalo
ISBN 0-8020-1881-5
ISBN microfiche 0-8020-0221-8

Printed in Japan

Note: All Japanese personal names in this
book with the exception of the author's
name follow Japanese usage, i.e., family
name first.

Contents

Foreword

Several works by Japanese authors on the Japanese national character or national culture have been published in English. One example is the summary version of the report of the National Character Study Committee, *The Japanese National Character*. The present translation of *Nihonjin no shinri* presents another view of the psychology of the Japanese people, one which became a best seller in Japan. It is hoped that this edition in English will be helpful to all who are interested in understanding the Japanese mind, for Professor Minami attempts to make the "inscrutable Japanese" scrutable. He has written a new preface for this edition, in which he points out the kinds of changes that have been taking place in Japan during the years since the original publication of his book. Perhaps symbolic of the great change in Japan is the popular use today of the expression *harenchi*, which literally means "shameless" but has come to mean the "groovy" thing to do. Japanese young people today seem to approve of many things which are undignified, according to traditional Japanese standards. Yet an insight into the traditional way of thinking remains basic to an understanding of the present generation of Japanese.

We are grateful to Albert Ikoma for his painstaking translation.

The Editors
East-West Center

Preface to the English Edition

When this book was first published in 1953, it was eight years after Japan's defeat. It was a year in which it looked as if we were going to build a peaceful nation as outlined in the new Japanese constitution. The Korean War ended that year, promising peace in Asia. Public telecasting was beginning to grow, bringing mass media culture to Japan. However, there were elements in Japanese human relations and in the standards influencing the Japanese mentality which retained a number of premodern features. This was true in spite of the changes taking place in the Japanese political and economic structure designed to put Japan on a new track after the war. What kinds of negative functions did these premodern elements perform in the modernization? Furthermore, how much had modern elements been able to grow within the feudalistic society in the hundred years since the Meiji restoration? The purpose of this book was to answer these and other related questions concerning the Japanese psychology seen in a historical perspective.

How has the Japanese mind changed in the sixteen years since the publication of this book? The political, economic, and cultural changes of these sixteen years are so drastic that perhaps we can call them revolutionary. However, these changes did not immediately elicit corresponding changes in the Japanese mentality. What follows is my attempt to predict how the Japanese mind is changing, following the themes I have described previously.

Concerning the Japanese concept of self, the Japanese have begun to lose interest in devoting themselves to the good of the society without much regard for themselves personally; they have begun to place individual interest first. These hypotheses are substantiated by a series of nationwide surveys on the life philosophy of the Japanese people conducted by the Committee for the Study of the Japanese National Character in the Japanese Ministry of Education. According to the findings of the survey made in 1953 the most popular philosophy was "to live a pure and just life by eliminating social injustices to the best of one's ability." However, this changed in the next fifteen years. According to the fourth survey, conducted in 1968, the most popular life philosophy was "to live one's life according to one's own tastes, without much regard for money and fame." This may support the hypothesis that the Japanese are beginning to place greater emphasis on individual and family leisure-time activities. Although people may not be able to put this new principle into practice immediately, it is becoming an important part of Japanese life.

The revolutionary transition from a philosophy based on hard work to one centered on leisure is manifested in Japanese life in the increasing popularity of television, bicycle racing, horse racing, and gambling.

What has been presented so far is closely related to the second topic of the book, the Japanese reaction to happiness and unhappiness. Today, in order to enrich our lives, we Japanese are buying paperback editions of best sellers, most of them books on how to do things. Books such as *How to Be a Successful White-Collar Worker, How to Succeed in Love, Marriage, and Sex*, and *Guidebook for Leisure-Time Activities* aim at satisfying the material wants of the Japanese, whose pursuit of happiness is now focused on leisure-time activities, These seem to embody the most practical cultural values for masses of people at the present time.

On the other hand, there are still many tear-jerking movies designed for housewives, soap operas on lost love, Platonic love, extramarital relations, separation of parents from children, and conflicts among three mothers (the mother who bore a child, the mother who raised the child, and the mother-in-law), and other dramas which depict the old family and human relationships. Furthermore, there are a number of popular songs which continue to play up sad lost love, parted love, secret love, and the dark fate of women. These unhappy themes, reflected in popular songs presented on television and in dramas, correspond to the reality of Japanese family life which is yet to be modernized. The conflicts among members of the family, alienation from family life, and *jyō hatsu* (young people leaving home as a result of being alienated from family life) indicate that the traditional Japanese family system has not really dissolved.

However, the Japanese feeling of unhappiness has been disappearing during the past fifteen years, particularly among the younger generation. The most popular television programs among the youth are programs characterized by *harenchi*, which literally means "shameless," although it has come to mean "the fashionable thing to do." These programs carry a number of stories about resistance to the existing code of ethics and moral standards and about the search for freedom. They include a number of action-oriented stories concerning sex, thrills, speed, and wild activities. Although adults criticize these programs as vulgar, the programs are welcomed by the younger generation. A similar trend can be observed in the songs popular with young people. Happiness in love and sex is pursued positively in these songs and programs. These trends are relatively recent, having started only two or three years ago, and they may indicate a shift in attitude from a negative to a positive approach to life, particularly among young people. These trends are perhaps also manifested in students' concern for politics and action today, which is becoming a worldwide phenomenon. Furthermore the folk songs written in the past several years in Japan have antiwar, peace, and other social protest themes.

There seems to be an increasing gap between the way the younger generation and adults live, think, and feel. This problem is not limited to education but is one of the most important problems Japanese society must face in the future.

The confrontations between generations may be an indication of younger people's rationalism in contrast to the older generation's irrationalism. This rationalism is considered a virtue among youth, and a person displaying it is described as "unemotional." Such rationalism and scientism is necessary for the "new man" living in the computer age.

Materialism is becoming popular as a reaction against the older generation's spiritualism. Increasing numbers of men and women are paying more attention to their clothing and appearance. This is manifested in current expressions such as *kakko ii*, "fine style" or "looks good." Even small children of three or four look at toys and say "kakko ii." The term is used for activities as well: all desirable action, such as heroic acts and attitudes, is referred to as being *kakko ii*. This may be seen as an expansion of materialism and sensualism and may be described as a materialization of cultural values.

Freedom of expression is beginning to spread to the areas of sexual mores, literature, and art. In the past decade or so, sensualism has begun to be publicly and socially accepted as legitimate.

In human relations the confrontation between the generations is becoming increasingly serious. Among older people, there still exist relationships characterized by *on* and *giri* and scandals which show misuse of *on* and *giri*. People in the middle and upper classes are beginning to spend considerably more than they did in prewar days for special occasions such as weddings and funerals. In this sense, in spite of the "rationalization" of life, the introduction of modern electrical gadgets to the home, and the development of material civilization, there seems to be a revival of the traditional way of life.

However, the modernization of human relations in various ways is part of an attempt younger people are making to rationalize their way of life. For example, they are not interested in festivals, religion, ethics, etiquette, and the code of conduct to be followed in the family, at school, or at work. This antitraditional trend is spreading rapidly in spite of the older generation's critical attitudes. As a result of urbanization, this proclivity is observed in mores which were traditionally under the jurisdiction of the family.

The conflict between generations is beginning to explode in various forms of struggle. The most extreme example can be seen in the university and high school students' political activity. What can one do to make life more meaningful in terms of its material as well as its spiritual aspects, using the existing conflict between the two generations as a point of departure? This is a problem for each individual Japanese which is shared equally by people all over the world.

I am grateful to the East-West Center for including my book among their translation projects. I am indebted to Albert R. Ikoma for his patient and conscientious work in translation. And I wish to thank the editorial staff of the University of Tokyo Press for their advice and assistance.

Hiroshi Minami
July 1971

Preface to the Original Edition

It is said that a fish is unaware of water although he spends his entire life in it. Since we Japanese were born, raised, and make a living among other Japanese, it is hard for us to see either the good or the bad characteristics of the Japanese.

Research and observations have been made on the Japanese "national character" both by Japanese and by foreigners, whose eyes reflect interesting portraits of the Japanese. Many analyses written by Japanese in the past were self-eulogizing, written to prove the excellence of the Japanese race, or showed the kind of self-praise which looks upon a pockmark as a dimple. On the other hand, when the war ended, impressions tinged with a self-tormenting inferiority complex showing a tendency to regard the Japanese as an inferior people became conspicuous. Either type is embarrassing.

The observations by foreigners, on the other hand, contain many laughable misconceptions. However, since they look from the outside, they often put a finger on things we ourselves do not notice, but because of differences in surroundings and deficiencies in their command of the Japanese language, it is hard for them to understand the motivation of the Japanese as they would that of their own countrymen.

Since research methods concerning the abstraction of a psychology of personality common to people belonging to one social group have become more advanced lately in both social psychology and anthropology, reports based on detailed research and observation have been made. *The Chrysanthemum and the Sword* (Boston: Houghton Mifflin, 1946), written by Ruth Benedict, is one example of such research. However, as is obvious in the Benedict book, theory is often superimposed on fact. When this happens, the theory makes sense as a whole but unreasonable interpretations often occur, and the theory is prone to fall into generalization.

In this book, I have attempted not to hypothesize or draw assumptions from a theory in regard to the psychology of the Japanese. Rather, I have briefly examined several points which I feel to be characteristic of the emotions, thought, and expressions of the Japanese and which are latent in the minds of the majority of us.

I then collected records, as much as possible from contemporary materials, which would distinctly substantiate these psychological traits. In some instances, I have outlined traditional psychological patterns which seem to have been the source of the current patterns. I felt that the stream which might be called the psychological tradition of the Japanese could be traced historically. Particularly because Japanese culture developed in islands separated from other cultures, the psychological tradition has not been fractured, in contrast to other countries, and the greater part of it has persisted until the present day.

I have selected the self-consciousness of the Japanese, their attitudes toward happiness and unhappiness, their way of thinking concerning metaphysical laws governing things, their attitudes in regard to the spirit and the body, and their social associations, particularly their vertical relationships. I have looked at the characteristics of human relationships and have attempted to discover the circumstances responsible for them.

This book neither discusses general considerations of the psychology of the Japanese nor explains it by using neat diagrams. Rather, it gathers material and tries to prepare the reader for discussion of the problem. I hope that the reader will make his own judgment, taking my ideas and materials into consideration.

At present, we Japanese are placed in the most serious crisis we have experienced since the dawn of our history. When Japan's independence is encroached upon and her people's independence is being lost, we must look at our society and people calmly and objectively.

In order to solve our urgent political problems, we must have an attitude that values each individual. Man should not be the victim of politics. Regardless of one's standpoint, whether reactionary or progressive, it is clear that undesirable characteristics springing from the psychological tradition of the Japanese still remain unsettled.

Although this book may seem to have been devoted only to picking out flaws in the Japanese character, these flaws are presented only as material for self-examination. Unpleasant and undesirable things are best found and cleaned up quickly. I have written this book hoping to help in accomplishing such a task, even if only to a slight extent.

In conclusion, may I again express my gratitude to Ebihara Mitsuyoshi and Nakajima Yoshikatsu of Iwanami Shoten and to Haraguchi Setsuko and Uchiyama Haruyo, who arranged source materials and manuscripts.

Hiroshi Minami
October 1953

Psychology of the Japanese People

1. The Japanese Self

Be Submissive to Authority

Hi-ri-hō-ken-ten is a traditional phrase in Japan. The five characters of the phrase were used by Kusunoki Masashige as a flag insignia. During the war, the phrase was frequently shouted by commanders of suicide units and was used as a flag insignia for such units. *Hi* signifies *injustice*, *ri* means *justice*, *hō* stands for *law*, *ken* means *authority*, and *ten* denotes the *Way of Heaven*. The whole phrase implies that injustice is subject to justice, justice to law, law to authority, and authority is subject only to the Way of Heaven. An admonishment to the warriors of the Tokugawa period says that these five concepts should always be kept in mind, otherwise "one would make mistakes on how things accord with reason."

The idea that although authority and power never transcend the Way of Heaven, they are more powerful than law and justice in human society and it is therefore unwise to oppose them, has been deeply instilled in the minds of the Japanese since the Tokugawa period. The lesson of submission was the first policy of the ruled; they learned to hide themselves by submitting, letting authority wrap and swallow them.

In the Tokugawa period, even Nishikawa Joken, who introduced Dutch natural science to Japan and could think rationally, said, "Inasmuch as the lower classes are not capable of playing a role in government but are subject to being ruled, they should not be rebellious even to the slightest degree but should conform."[1]

To the leaders of the Meiji government, the inculcation of such unconditional submission to authority seemed one of the best ways

---

1. Nishikawa Joken, *Hyakushō bukuro* [Lot of the Peasant] (1721).

to uphold their power. Long before the promulgation of the Imperial Rescript on Education in 1879, a minister of home affairs, Itō Hirobumi, commented that "to have many men who discuss politics is not fortunate for the people."[2] He proposed an educational policy which would suppress any criticism of authority. It is a well-known fact that Itō aimed at the cultivation of submissiveness by designating loyalty to the Emperor as the highest virtue. Such submissiveness began with elementary education: "Abide by the word of the Emperor always! Worship their Imperial Majesties every day!"

However, a submissive spirit is created by imbuing the minds of the people with a terror of vested authority by using words and violence rather than by teaching virtues. To the Japanese, authority, which has been seen and heard as "something long" and "something thick," is the government official, the policeman, and the military man.

The policeman was utilized most frequently for the cultivation of a submissive spirit beginning in early childhood. In large cities a scolding such as "If you don't listen to me, I will call a policeman!" is seldom heard now. However, in farming villages of the Tōhoku area, old women still scold children saying, "I'll report you to a policeman!"[3] And there are still many adults, not only in farming villages, who fear policemen.

The National Public Opinion Research Institute of the Prime Minister's Office made a survey, *Public Opinion in Regard to the Culture of Policemen* (*Keisatsukan no kyōyō ni kansuru yoron chōsa*, 1953). Reactions to being summoned to a police station to serve as a reference clearly reveal fear of the police even at the present time. "I was called in as a reference. I was very frightened because they threatened me unsparingly. I was really scared; it was . . . really unpleasant." (A female restaurant worker in her mid-twenties from Tochigi Prefecture.) "In the first place, no policeman uses decent Japanese.

---

2. Itō Hirobumi, *Kyōikugi* [Discussion on the Problem of Education] (1879).
3. Ōmura Ryō, "Nōson no sekentei" ["The Public Appearance of the Farming Village"], *Tōyō Bunka* 12 (1953).

The police station is a terrible place." (A female office worker in her thirties from Akita Prefecture.) The fear of the police, that is, the fear of being wrapped in "something long," becomes the basis of a submissive spirit.

"The main task of a policeman is to give scoldings. People are scolded, but they must be good at knowing how to be scolded. If one makes an excuse, one gives an unfavorable impression. The best thing to do is to admit one's wrongdoing and apologize for whatever one has done wrong."[4] This passage is quoted from a recently published book entitled *How to Come in Contact with Others* in which the art of living is explained. In the first eight rules the writer concludes that "to apologize humbly" is the best way to come into contact with government officials. In view of the fact that a book with such an approach is still in print, it seems that the idea of a submissive spirit still remains in people's minds.

Along with the policeman, the government official plays a role in educating people to fear and submit. Even today, many people fear any inquiry conducted by a government official. This can be seen when social research is carried out by nonofficial researchers or when public opinion surveys are made by newspapers.

"In a farming village in Iwate Prefecture, I was asked by a farmer, 'Is this by order of the government? . . . How shall I write? . . . Is this by order of the government? Is this by order of the U.S.A.?' At the same time he wonders, 'How should I write?' "[5] Thus, "the standard of judgment in answering questions for research on farmers is identical with the philosophy of life which says, 'Keep deities at a respectful distance lest you offend them' and 'Be submissive to authority.' To put it concretely, it is most likely that answers are anticipated which would satisfy the bossy people of the village."[6]

Such submissiveness to the government and government officials

---

4. Shimizu Masami, *Hito ni sessuru hō* [How to Come in Contact with Others] (Tokyo: Hakuyōsha, 1952).
5. Ōmura, "Farming Village."
6. Ibid.

stems not only from fear but also from avarice; it is submissiveness accompanied by adulation. The writer of *How to Come in Contact with Others* plainly undertakes to spread such submissiveness. He advises readers, "Respect government officials. This is not an idea derived from feudalistic thought. The government official has his own pride of position. It is none of my business whether or not you call this feudalistic thinking. It is the problem of the other party. All you have to do is to comply with that pride."[7]

Adulation springing from a wish to take advantage of government officials brings about the best results at the characteristic Japanese banquet. As a result, "a banquet to which a government official is invited ... whatever its purpose may be, is smoothly carried out only by showing him respect. Even if it is just a social gathering, the guest will become friendly with the host later."[8]

The submissiveness derived from avarice is only a facade; at heart the person is able to make fun of the government official. However, although initially superficial, when a person is surrounded by such constant obedience to authority, submission becomes unconsciously implanted in his mind. It is inevitable to fall into the habit of obedience to authority as long as a person keeps in mind rules such as "Apologize humbly," "Do not make excuses," "Be grateful to government officials," "Be sympathetic," "Be likable," "Do not treat a government official like your friend," "Never treat a government official as a public servant," and "Get acquainted with government officials."

Needless to say, in the army complete submissiveness was instilled in a short time. Young men were transformed into monsters of self-abasement, humiliation, and shrewdness by subjecting them to fear of violence in the name of punishment and by presenting the lure of avarice in the name of promotion.

"Barracks are the home of those who share joys and sorrows, life

---

7. Shimizu, *Contact with Others*.
8. Ibid.

and death. The purpose of barracks life is to cultivate the military spirit, to get the men accustomed to the military codes, and to unite them." These principles from the *Book of Internal Affairs of the Military* (*Guntai naimu sho*) are rephrased by Sōda, a university-graduate soldier depicted in *The Vacuum Zone* by Noma Hiroshi: "Barracks are a space about a half furlong square encircled by regulations and fences, within which an abstract society is built up by forcible pressures. The human beings there are deprived of all human elements and made into soldiers. . . . Certainly there exists no air in a barracks. They are emptied by forceful power. No, they're not vacuum tubes but places where vacuum tubes are manufactured. They are a vacuum zone. A man living there is deprived of a certain nature and society and is made into a soldier."[9] In this vacuum zone, a soldier with habits of nonresistance and absolute obedience is manufactured.

In a discussion meeting for the study of the Japanese military, officers of the former army spoke about methods of teaching submissiveness using violence. "Violence was used to implant the idea of absolute obedience. When a senior officer inquired as to why a soldier had done a certain thing, if the soldier explained his action, the senior officer beat him, telling him not to make excuses. If the soldier remained silent, the senior officer hit him, condemning his silence. He was beaten regardless of whether he gave a reason or remained silent. The best thing to do was to say 'Yes, sir, Yes, sir' repeatedly."[10]

In brief, there arises the idea that to be obedient, saying yes all the time, is one way to avert punishment. This is, in a sense, to be a human being and yet not to be a human being, for one has to be a spiritless automaton without a particle of self.

The young men who thought when they enlisted that they might

---

9. Noma Hiroshi, *Shinkū chitai* [The Vacuum Zone] (Tokyo: Kawade Shobō, 1952).
10. Iizuka Kōji, *Nihon no guntai* [The Japanese Military] (Tokyo: Tokyo Daigaku Shuppanbu, 1950).

be able to find some human warmth in the midst of bitterness gradually despaired. "My comrades whom I have thought highly of have begun to reveal what they really are. I am beaten at the rate of twice a day. There is not even one man in the barracks who seems to be human. I myself think as if I were not a human being."[11] Soldiers, gradually deprived of humanity, became living corpses, and if a soldier tried to recover his humanity he was beaten until he was nearly dead. "Last Sunday, I could not help but shed tears when I wrote a letter to my mother in the lavatory. Although I wrote to my mother that I was fine, my true feeling is as if I were dead. If a second-year soldier found me writing a letter like this, I'm sure I would be killed."[12]

In the navy, things were no different. *The Final Day of the Battleship Yamato* gives an authentic account of an old sailor's beating by a deck officer. "There is no end to finding fault with foot movements, salutes, language, order, and other details, so sailors avoid entering the gun room. . . . An old sailor was thrashed by harsh voices, and he repeated a dull motion. . . . A growling billy-club hit his back, followed by the dull sounds of blows; he fell down, pale cheeks crawling along the floor."[13]

Such violence was aimed at developing absolute submission in the men. This can easily be observed in a conversation between the author of the *Battleship Yamato* and an officer regarding the propriety of beating sailors.

"Do you know of a good officer who wouldn't administer a beating if he found something wrong?"

"There could be. I thought it was right not to beat them both for me and for the sailors."

---

11. Committee for Editing Notes of Dead Japanese Student Soldiers, *Kike wadatsumi no koe* [Listen to the Voices of the Sea] (Tokyo: University of Tokyo Press, 1952).

12. Ibid.

13. Yoshida Mitsuru, *Senkan Yamato no saigo* [The Final Day of the Battleship Yamato] (Tokyo: Sōgensha, 1952).

"Where are you now? Are you out of the service?"

"I'm on board a warship, sir."

"In a battlefield, no matter how good and understanding an officer is, he's got to be tough or else he is useless."

"I don't agree with you, sir."

For a while they glared at each other.

"You have a point. I've understood it. Let's put it to the test, and see whether my men or yours are braver. There is no guarantee that your men won't look down on you, thinking that since their officer is a nice man, he wouldn't order them to run through a rain of shells."[14]

Such constraint by means of violence gradually implants a habit of absolute submission in the minds of soldiers. It is a frame of mind in which personal thoughts or desires are suppressed and a person makes himself available whenever an order is given by his superior. In other words, in military life an individual suppresses his spontaneity and creates a habit of receiving orders and responding like a machine. One student soldier described the conditions this way: "Throughout my experiences, I would say that the bitterness of military life lay not in the excessive physical burdens of daily living but in the tension of standing by ready to comply with orders given by someone else and my incessant effort to perceive the will of others, mainly my senior comrades, to the point where my own intentions were suffocated."[15]

Through such a process, many a soldier became a human machine, not feeling the suffocation of his own will. Of course, this nonhumanity took on a different guise in each individual. For instance, many a second or third son from a farming village had already cultivated a habit of submission in family relationships before he enlisted, so he readily complied with the demands of military life.

According to the survey of farming villages in Iwate Prefecture

14. Ibid.
15. Ōmura, "Farming Village."

cited earlier, "especially the second or third son and his wife, who live with the head of the family, move slowly. These slow movements are often mistaken for easygoing behavior, but they are not actually easygoing. Such slow movements seem to be only the revelation of their careful attention to circumstances and their accordant behavior. They thus serve the head of the family, sacrificing themselves until they are allowed to set up a separate family. The allocation of property depends on the degree of their service. . . . Before enlistment they have already done duty as conscripts in the agricultural society." Thus, "farm youths, who were often said to be very unsophisticated and naive, could raise themselves to the position of selected superior private by preserving appearances for the senior soldiers and by living up to other people's expectations."

The spiritual discipline necessary to achieve submission in the army was extolled by many people during the war as the ideal not only for the army but also for schooling and social education. Even after the war, at the present time, there are still many people who condone habitual obedience to authority.

In a survey done by the National Public Opinion Research Institute of the Prime Minister's Offices, *A Survey of Public Opinion on Social Education* (*Shakai kyōiku ni tsuite no yoron chōsa*, March 1953), the percentage of people who affirmed the attitude of obedience to authority is shown in the following table.

Age	Male	Female
16–19	17%	14%
20–24	30	22
25–29	27	28
30–39	38	35
40–49	35	38
50–58	40	43

Even if we cannot accept the figures as they stand, generally speaking, the tendency to submission seems to be widely supported by people over thirty.

Service above Self

A submissive spirit not only makes mechanical submission to authority a habit but also hinders the growth of an unrestricted self. Conversely, it is possible to fortify the habit of submission by restraining the growth of the self. "Be wrapped in something long" is related to the time-honored term, "no self."

Books of *shingaku* (popular ethics), which taught a philosophy of life to the masses of the Tokugawa period, always encouraged the people to have no self. The purport of the term is not to act as one pleases, forgetting who one is, but to serve one's superiors dutifully. The purpose of *shingaku* was to make the masses into slaves who were selfless, unselfish, and faithful in assigned work. The *Sequel to Kyūō's Moral Discourses* says, "If one had no selfish motives but only the supreme virtues, there would be no self. . . . If he serves selflessly, he does not know what service is. If he knows what service is, he has a self. If you think that you work diligently, it is not true service."[16]

Whether one realizes it or not, the concept of no self is identical with the spirit of service above self, where every spontaneous impulse is rejected as selfishness. Therefore, filial piety consists of thinking "only of your parents but not of yourself. This is what I call 'no self.' You should be grateful to this feeling of 'no self,' for because you do not act as you please, things will, conversely, turn out right for you."[17]

In *shingaku* the highest virtue for a townsman was to sacrifice himself. "To think of merits and demerits is egotism. If a person could surpass egotism, he would be a man of good nature, and merit would follow him in accordance with the Way of Heaven."[18]

In the same sense, among warriors the spirit of service above self

16. Kyūō, *Zoku Kyūō dōwa* [Sequel to Kyūō's Moral Discourses] (1835).
17. Ibid.
18. Fuse Shōō, *Shōō dōwa* [Shōō's Moral Discourses] (1814–1846).

meant that "my body and my life are not my possessions. I would consider it an honor to offer myself whenever the lord is in need of me."[19]

In a book entitled *Complete Works for the Exposition of the Way of the Subject* published during the Second World War, this spirit of the people in relation to the Emperor is explained in exactly the same way as in the way of the warrior: "The primary duty is to sacrifice my very body and mind for the sake of the Emperor. . . . It should be mentioned that our lives, though ours, are yet not ours."[20]

The discussion quoted earlier from *The Japanese Military* emphasized that the military spirit is identical with the spirit of no self; therefore, "any assigned work should at that very moment be fulfilled faithfully in the proper manner. It is disloyal to think of yourself."[21] The self is thus denied as a symbol of disloyalty. This gives rise to the logic that any action should be carried out not on one's own spontaneous and personal responsibility but passively, in response to the order of a superior, that is, through absolute submission to the order of the Emperor. Hence, it follows naturally that the noncommissioned officers and soldiers who were sentenced to death or were prosecuted as minor war criminals raised their voices in anger. In fact, a noncommissioned officer who participated in the execution of the crew members of a B-29 said, "Yes, I did indeed kill the crew members. However, I did not myself conspire nor did I voluntarily do it. It was done by order of my superior. The order was absolute. It was equal to the voice of the sacred and inviolable Commander-in-Chief."[22]

Indeed in the army every spontaneous action was prohibited, and

19. Daidōji Yūzan, *Budō shoshinshū* [Basic Principles of the Way of the Warrior] (1834).
20. Sonda Hideharu, *Shinmin no michi kaisetsu taisei* [Complete Works for the Exposition of the Way of the Subject] (Tokyo: Taimeidō, 1942).
21. Iizuka, *Japanese Military.*
22. Iizuka Kōji, *Arekara shichinen* [Seven Years Have Passed] (Tokyo: Kōbunsha, 1953).

everyday life was framed by forces outside the individual. Of course, at the beginning of military life this frame was a constraint, and a person was still aware of submission to orders. However, over time, submissive action customarily and mechanically repeated without question or criticism became automatic. The soldier forgot that he was constrained and came to have no self; a habit of submission, doing away with self, was instilled in him.

In military terms, a good soldier is one whose reaction time is shorter than others': he receives an order and puts it into action immediately. The term *meirei ikka* (blow of command) signifies a habit of automatic and immediate fulfillment of an order. In the army, therefore, as a lower-grade officer mentioned, it was very important "to reform one's critical attitude thoroughly": "although soldiers from the military preparatory school immediately comply with orders, high school graduates do not submit very easily once they have made a living in the outside world."[23] Military life, because of the effort made to eliminate the critical mind cultivated in the outside world, deserves the name "vacuum zone."

Once a habit of submission is formed, it becomes natural to submit to anything. Compliance with orders begins to feel like simply acting in accordance with the demands of nature. In brief, "duty becomes internalized and appears subjective and spontaneous."[24]

Thus, in proportion to the intensification of the habit of submission, behavior outside of the frame is perceived as mental pain. In other words, one is bound to act mechanically in accordance with the orders he is given. For instance, a regulation to go to the worshipping place set up in the preparatory course of the military academy resulted in a habit. "At first, it was, so to speak, a pain and I regarded it as an effort. However, as it became a habit, I felt quite unpleasant all day long whenever I did not go there. . . . I therefore went at night when I could not go in the morning."[25]

---

23. Iizuka, *Japanese Military.*
24. Ibid.
25. Ibid.

The habit of submission induces a feeling of uneasiness and dissatisfaction in a person removed from a prearranged living pattern. This is a type of psychological "addiction," for if a person is removed from a schedule of mechanical living, he shows withdrawal symptoms: he has to act in accordance with the schedule throughout the day or he is unable to be at ease mentally. Thus, a human being becomes an addict of regulation and submission; he is thrown into ecstacies by being bound by regulation. As a graduate of the military academy said, "There are men who claim that it would be far better to be given a blow than to be scolded shilly-shally."[26]

It is masochistic to feel pleasure in violence inflicted upon one as a penalty for violating a regulation. Pleasure stemming from the chastisement imposed when one attempts to free oneself from confinement is also masochistic. Japanese moral education, as I will show later, concentrated on implanting such an attitude, which might be called "Japanese masochism," in students' minds.

During the war such discipline was not only demanded and encouraged in the army but also in school and at home. A businessman who was once a leader of the "Campaign for Service to the State through Industry" said, "Inasmuch as father, master, and superior forced a young man to follow them, not letting him have his own way but imposing strict discipline upon him, obedience became a habit; he was brought up to be as unmoved and steadfast as iron forged into steel."[27]

This habit, along with the habit of submission or no self, led to attitudes reflected in the phrases "Keep deities at a respectful distance lest you offend them," "You are always right," and a "please-all policy."

---

26. Ibid.
27. Ōkura Kunihiko, *Musubi no sangyō* [Industrial Activity Based on the Spirit of *Musubi*] (Tokyo: Dainihon Sangyō Hōkoku Kai, 1942).

Keep Deities at a Respectful Distance

When absolute submission to order is intensified, it becomes an overwhelming passivity, a desire for peace at any price. Submission is shown in toadyism towards one's superiors, while negativism appears in a please-all attitude, not only towards one's superiors but also towards one's colleagues and inferiors.

Tōkyū-jutsu, a system of astrology which used to have many adherents in the gay quarters and among entertainers in Tokyo, divined fortunes employing the date of birth and the art of self-improvement. It urged a please-all policy, as this quotation from Itō Hirobumi shows: "Prince Itō always practiced a please-all policy, thinking it best to be noncommittal, for this never makes an enemy but is loved by all. To say something eccentric or to argue for argument's sake incurs the distaste of others. . . . 'In this world, that's right; that's right, you are right. Is that right? I don't know for sure.' There have been many who have always kept this poem in mind, have put it into practice, and have made themselves prominent."[28]

Following this advice, one agrees to any opinion of others, saying, "You are right," but not expressing one's own opinion, saying, "I don't know for sure." This is merely an expansion from the habit of submission to the habit of negativity. A person soon assumes an attitude devoid of spontaneity in all situations. From the point of view of foreigners, the Japanese seem to be reserved and retiring. In many cases this is evidence of negativism stemming from the habit of submission.

Spontaneous expression of opinion is rejected as obstinacy and sophism. In *How to Come in Contact with Others*, the author instructs the reader how to come in contact with his seniors: "Be reverent

28. Yōshin-dō and Shōyō-dō, *Tōkyu-jutsu kōwa* [A System of Astrology] (Tokyo: Eirakudō, 1912).

towards your seniors, always assuming the attitude that you learn from them. Never think that you are on an equal footing with them. Let them feel superiority over you."[29] As a person becomes tamed by the "you are right" habit, which he manifests not only toward his seniors but toward everyone, he eventually gives negative answers such as "I don't know" and "I don't understand" to everything, despite having his own opinion, or else he remains silent.

Especially in farming villages, even now, remaining silent or assuming an attitude of "you are right" prevails. According to a peddler who hawked his wares around the farming villages in the Tōhoku area, a farmer of a certain village "only echoed me and did not utter a word of his own opinion. Even when I showed him a kimono with cross stripes, obviously too quiet for a young girl, saying, 'It becomes your daughter,' the farmer echoed me, answering, 'It does.' When I showed a working coat with very short sleeves, saying, 'With this you can work comfortably,' he nodded back to me, saying only, 'That's right, yes indeed.' I really wondered if there were any chance of his expressing opposition to another's word."[30]

However, the please-all policy appears only in a person's speech; in actual behavior one is not so agreeable. "Although the farmer answered as if convinced, he seemed not to have assented fully in spite of nodding back to me, for he knew what and how to buy when it was actually time to buy. . . . When I observed associations in the village, the people were more than necessarily courteous and polite."[31]

In other words, the please-all policy has a phase of persistence in one's own will while avoiding a clash of opinions. At this point the habit of negativity, together with the habit of submission, is useful for preventing difficulties in life as well as for preserving the security of the self.

---

29. Shimizu, *Contact with Others.*
30. Ōmura, "Farming Village."
31. Ibid.

Since both submission and affirmation originally spring from a wish for security, no self is, in fact, a form of egoism and is a useful expediency, although it is not self-assertion in the modern sense. Hence, as I will show later, after the surrender in 1945, when the rule of submission was about to collapse, the egoism that had been hidden in submission gushed out, and terrible conflicts motivated by avarice arose. Submission and negativity are in a sense like a smoke screen for egocentricity: they serve to conceal and intensify it.

Live as You Please

Submission and its concomitant, negativity, however, cannot make a complete slave of a man because he cannot stamp out the self latent at the core of his personality. And when the frame of submission is by chance weakened or removed, the confined self begins to proclaim its existence in various ways.

In Japan, since a thoroughly modern society did not exist even after the Meiji period, there was no social foundation on which the majority of the Japanese could establish a free and individual self. Fukuzawa Yukichi explained this long ago in his *Outline of the Discourses on Civilization*. "Throughout history Japan has claimed to be a nation of loyalty and courage, and the warrior seems to have been openhearted and unrestrained. However, the qualities of openheartedness and unrestraint were motivated neither by his righteous indignation nor by his disposition to recognize himself as a man and enjoy freedom based on the idea that he is free, at his own disposal. They sprang from either an external inducement or an external aid."[32] These external factors, according to Fukuzawa, were ancestry, family name, lord, father, social status, and so forth, and as a result, "Japanese warriors did not have any individuality."[33]

32. Fukuzawa Yukichi, *Bunmeiron no gairyaku* [Outline of the Discourses on Civilization] (1875).
33. Ibid.

Fukuzawa was one of the first Japanese to advocate individual freedom. He felt that "man's independence, freedom, and self-reliance are significant. If the meaning of these concepts were mistaken, virtue would not be cultivated, knowledge would not be acquired, families would not be governed, states would not be founded, and independence of the state could not be expected."[34]

However, sound individualism and egoism, from the Meiji period to the present, have never flourished among the Japanese, contrary to Fukuzawa's expectation. These existed among some thinkers and politically aware people but, as I have already stated, they had no bearing on the majority of the Japanese. The masses, however, sought a chance for self-assertion at any cost. Under absolute submission to authority, self-assertion took two forms.

The first was to cherish mercenary and egoistic wishes under the mask of submission. In this case, self-assertion amounts to cherishing self-interest. Instead of a free self, only a self enslaved to avarice remains. A lance corporal depicted in *The Vacuum Zone* brags about his slavish smartness: "A really smart soldier like me never fails to free himself from field operations, become a lance corporal, wait for the day of discharge, and return home with the rank of corporal as a discharge souvenir."[35]

Such egoism, however, may have been a kind of resistance to submission and oppression. In a society where honesty is the loser, to be a smart soldier is contrary to being a faithful soldier, and the corporal obviously had the ability to cope with the situation. Presumably, there must have been very few soldiers who were not overcome by the temptation to become "smart soldiers."

Likewise, most of the graduates of the military academy wanted inwardly to become "smart officers," though outwardly they assumed an attitude of ignoring scores. "Merits or demerits were judged with one's attainments at the time of commencement. Even

---

34. Ibid.
35. Noma, *Vacuum Zone*.

after appointment to an office, promotion was made in accordance with these attainments . . . so we did think of making a good score. But if I had expressed this plainly, I would have been scorned for paying attention to petty details. The difficulty lay in knowing how to combine two contradictory things cleverly: the reverse side, getting a good score, with the face. Therefore, I had to study without giving the impression that I studied hard."[36] In this situation, submission paradoxically incurs self-interest. Herein lies the duality common to the psychology of the Japanese people.

Men framed in a firm and strict order, unless they explicitly deny order, are apt to breathe within the frame of the order without infringing on its regulations or acting contrary to them. They become skillful in the use of submission and cleverness, that is, in knowing "how to combine two contradictory things cleverly."

The more submissive one becomes, the more necessary and important cleverness becomes. Then, as a person thinks of his clever compliance, a reverse reaction makes him much more submissive, and this reaction restricts him from acting any more clever. A confession of a soldier in *The Vacuum Zone* clearly reveals such a state of mind: "Is there anyone who is really fond of the army? If anyone were found after searching all over the country, I would indeed like to see him. . . . But every soldier, contrary to his tongue, has a patriotic sentiment in the depths of his mind."[37]

Actually, I would not say that every soldier had such patriotic sentiments; however, the truth is that a sense of submission and service and an aspiration for liberty have from time to time either been blended into a relatively harmonious principle of cleverness or have created a dilemma.

The *Hagakure*, a highly eulogized sacred book of death, not only propounded absolute sacrifice, "the way of the warrior is to know how to die," but also made the following amazing statement: "Life

---

36. Iizuka, *Japanese Military.*
37. Noma, *Vacuum Zone.*

is indeed short. One should live as one pleases. It is foolish to suffer from not doing as one likes in this dreamlike world. This should be kept secret and never be told to the youth for it is harmful to them. I am fond of sleep. I feel that I should confine myself at home, in accordance with my present lot, and live in bed."[38]

Yamamoto Jinemon Jōchō, the author of the *Hagakure*, was a loyal vassal of Nabeshima Mitsushige, the lord of the Saga clan. When restrained from self-immolation by a state interdict, he expressed his true feelings in the *Hagakure*. In it, the secret of the warrior, the principle of cleverness and self-interest under the rigid feudal system, is clearly visible. It is quite an interesting example of the type of confession never revealed by inquiry but in casual talk.

Even a One-Inch Worm Has a Half-Inch Soul

The compulsion to submit not only creates self-interest as a means of negative resistance but it also, on some occasions, induces a positive, rebellious spirit against the coercive power. There is, however, no certainty that this opposition will always take the form of political resistance or a revolution. Especially in Japanese society, the state's encouragement of submission and coercion even after the Meiji period prevented the development of social and human revolutions. As a result, opposition tended to be expressed as egoistic self-assertion rather than as a direct denial of authority.

Self-assertion based on egocentricity leads not to the establishment of a modern self but to selfish conduct based on individual autonomy. And this selfishness, contrary to self-assertion founded on the recognition of the self of others and on a regard for humanity, stems from a distrust of and disdain for man.

A free self is originally formed by means of a social revolution where people get rid of submission and coercion and liberate them-

---

38. Yamamoto Jinemon Jōchō, *Hagakure* [In the Shade of Leaves] (1716).

selves. However, in the case of Japan, the authority of the state was brought down not by the hand of the people but by the hand of an enemy country in war, and "freedom" was bestowed by the occupying forces of the conqueror. It was a passive freedom and an ordered freedom, given in exchange for surrender.

For the majority of the Japanese, therefore, resistance against power ends up with a blast of egoism and is not directed toward social and human revolution. The realization of the self was not the result of overthrowing the power which had forced the principle of "no self" upon them. When their trust and fear of that power were eliminated by the forces of a foreign country, people became distrustful of the old power and of those who had been connected with it.

This distrust developed into a distrust of all men, and a man was driven to egocentricity: only he himself is trustworthy and only his interests are important. Once an advocate of the principle of cleverness within the frame of submission, he became as advocate of egoism within the frame of a bestowed freedom.

Resistance against power and authority is first manifested in various indirect criticisms. Examples of this are the rumors, jokes, and popular songs which incur no punishment and revenge. There is a traditional army counting song: "Number one, the man who voluntarily joins the army, which everyone hates, is a genuine fool; he who renews his enlistment is the fool of all fools. . . . Number six, sick of the army, we must even do absolutely ridiculous things in the name of order."

Thus, in the army a counting song was one means of venting dissatisfaction. However, as a more direct means, threats and violence were imposed upon inferiors to pass along one's discontent with the threats and violence exerted by one's superiors. Dissatisfaction flows downward like a waterfall. "Officers beat noncommissioned officers; noncommissioned officers thrash superior privates; superior privates strike soldiers; soldiers, having no one to wreak their anger on, let fly at horses. . . . When the horses in a stable are

wild or have bruises, you know that punishment is inflicted extensively in that cavalry squadron."[39]

An outlet for discontent, whether verbal or physical, is a psychological safety valve tacitly permitted in the existing order. A typical
example of such a safety valve is a rumor about the Emperor
or the Imperial Household. Such rumors spread widely among
the people until the defeat. The content of these rumors might have
fallen under the charge of *lèse majesté* if announced publicly, yet
they were widely circulated as part of everyone's daily conversation.

In those who are aware of the confrontation of their inner self
with authority, resistance is found in the conflicts with the
submissive part of the self, despite their superficial submission to
authority. This is evident in the note left by a student soldier who
died at war.

> Do I try to spare my life? I do, perhaps. No matter how good
> one may be at mouthing an understanding of totalitarianism or
> the relationship between the whole and individuals, what re-
> mains finally is self. Speaking extremely, I dare say there is no
> individual who is not prone to individualism.
>
> It is somehow queer that ever since I enlisted I have become
> antagonistic and I have striven not to be picked on by anyone. . . .
> However, I have at heart really despised what is called the military
> spirit. The more I was told to get rid of worldly desires, the more
> I clung to them, for I felt that if I were to lose them I would be
> worthless. If others had looked at me, they would have felt that
> I was leading a double life with the greatest circumspection.[40]

When the war was near its end and authority began to crumble,
such resistance of the self exploded in the form of direct criticism

39. Iizuka, *Japanese Military.*
40. Committee for Compiling Notes of Student Soldiers Killed in World War II,
    eds., *Haruka naru yamakawani* [To Far-off Mountains and Rivers] (Tokyo:
    Mikasa Shobō, 1952).

of authority, though it had been limited previously to a form of indirect self-assertion.

A student enlistee, who died as a Kaiten suicide submariner, boldly criticized the navy's authority in his will addressed to his mother. "The naval officers utterly disappointed me. I am disgusted with professional naval men. . . . Their so-called naval tradition or common sense is to face us and regulate us with extreme formalism. It is nothing but a formalistic and bigoted convention which has been laboriously made up by insular, narrow-minded people."[41]

When the end of the war was near, resistance to orders became visible, not only among soldiers but also among officers. In spite of the regulation that an appeal should not be made by more than two persons, many officers banded together, criticized an order of their superior, and openly declared that they wouldn't mind taking direct action if necessary. When the buildings of a regiment in Tokyo were burned down in an air raid, a company commander was blamed for it and was ordered to hold an unreasonable fire drill. In consequence, discontent with the regimental commander exploded among the officers. "A certain second lieutenant, blowing up in anger, said that he would throw shells into the regimental headquarters if the mainland were to become a battlefield. I was also mad and protested. The words of the battalion commander, who acted as a mediator and encouraged me to cast away my uniform if necessary, were a great relief to me. It was because of the uniform that I had to suffer. He encouraged me to do as I pleased, with a suggestion to take off my shoulder straps if necessary."[42] As seen in this example, even the battalion commander, in cooperation with the others, showed an antagonistic attitude toward the power of the regimental commander.

In the navy, the officers of the *Yamato* furiously protested the conclusion of the board from the gunnery academy that the cause of their crushing defeat in an air raid was lack of training.

---

41. Ibid.
42. Iizuka, *Japanese Military.*

An epithet was written in bold strokes right under the conclud-
ing words of a war admonishment forwarded from the gunnery
academy: "You big fool, Captain Shirabuchi." (This was followed
by an empty page.) . . . A tag was attached to it which said, "What
was lacking was not training but enthusiasm and ability in scientific study. . . . What do you mean by lack of training, under circumstances like this?" All of the first and second lieutenants signed
their names under it. Nobody was reprimanded or punished for
such rude behavior. That war admonishment was circulated in
absolute silence among the staff officers.

"The three biggest fools in the world, samples of good-for-
nothingness," said the young officers disparagingly, "are the Great
Wall of China, the Pyramids, and *Yamato!*" Even on board they
did not hesitate to shout things like "The only way to save the
navy is to shoot every officer above the rank of lieutenant commander!"[43]

On the *Yamato*, as signs of a sortie grew conspicuous, the agonies
and sufferings prevalent among the young officers caused a large
number of disputes. Since a decisive defeat was only a question
of time, scuffles finally arose between the officers who were naval
academy graduates and the college-graduate officers, who tried to
understand the significance of death.

All of the academy-graduate lieutenants unanimously said, "To
die for the sake of the country and for the sake of His Majesty,
. . . isn't that a sufficient reason for death?"

The college-graduate officers retorted, flaring up in anger, "We
know how to die for the sake of sovereign and country! But what
is it related to?"

"That's only a paper argument! Useless! No, it's a rather harmful sophism! Aren't you glad to die with the floating chrysanthe-

---

43. Yoshida, *The Final Day of the Battleship Yamato.*

mum crest of the suicide corps on your chest, saying, 'Long live the Emperor?' "

"No, not only for that! Something, something more is needed!"

The argument ended in a rain of fists and a scene of scuffles.[44]

Thus, in the last stage of the war, there arose a tendency toward resistance against the military authority, which planned imprudent strategies or issued reckless orders, by members of the military from soldiers to high-ranking officers. When the war was ended, the military authority was unmasked at a stroke and, at the same time, many remonstrances and condemnations were made public by soldiers and officers. The behavior of high-ranking officers who had pressed submission upon them was harshly criticized, especially in memoranda written by noncommissioned officers who were unjustly treated as condemned war criminals.

> In prison I met Lieutenant General So-and-so, Colonel So-and-so, and others and lived together with them; however, without uniforms and ornaments, they are hardly objects for my observation in their speech and conduct. . . . Japanese servicemen, especially after the Manchurian Incident and, later, after the occupation of the South Seas area, became more rotten at heart than merchants whose work it is to seek after profits daily. . . . Where are the high-sounding words like "loyalty" and "sacrificial spirit" which they always uttered?[45]

Another condemned war criminal censured unjust trials which imposed light sentences on high-ranking war criminals. He believed that his life was more important than the lives of corrupt senior officers.

> Several colonels, lieutenant colonels, and company officers may be sentenced to death, which they deserve as long as they did

---

44. Ibid.

45. Committee for Editing Notes, *Listen to the Voices of the Sea.*

whatever they are accused of. If I were to be saved by their death, I'm quite convinced that my survival, from a nationalistic point of view, would be more useful. I'm confident that even if these servicemen, who uttered flowery words with no meaning and played with their so-called spiritual words, who were nothing but avaricious men desiring fame and vanity, were to lead in the future a life similar to that of the past, they would not do anything useful for the country.[46]

Superior Private Kimura Hisao, a student of the Faculty of Economics, Kyoto University, was twenty-eight when he was executed in Singapore in May 1946. Discarding absolute obedience to his superiors for the first time, he exclaimed in this memorandum that his life was several times more useful than that of his superiors. Here the true being in a man, a man who has discovered a self undaunted by authority, can be clearly seen.

With self-assertion, however, distrust and disappointment in human beings as a whole must have been felt by every war criminal. A sergeant who was also executed expressed distrust and disappointment in man, questioning and criticizing the authority of high-ranking officers as well as the Emperor.

Generally speaking, there is hardly a decent high-ranking officer. . . . We were despised, fooled, deceived, entrapped, and treated harshly. . . . Never again join the army! Whom did we fight for? For the sake of the Emperor, that is what we believed, but it seems not to have been so. The Emperor has not saved my life. I faithfully obeyed any distasteful order as the Emperor's order. And I always endeavored to bear the spirit of the Imperial Mandate in mind. . . . But I can no longer believe in anything. To bear the unbearable and to endure the unendurable means that I must die? I'll be killed. So a sentence has been passed on me. I will have abided by His Majesty's order up to the moment of my death.

---

46. Ibid.

So I'm leveling with you. What I owed you for was only seven or eight cigarettes distributed at the front in China and some candy given at the field hospital. Those were certainly expensive cigarettes. I am paying for them with my life and have undergone prolonged suffering for them. I will never be deceived by soothing words. I'm being honest with you. If I were to be reborn a Japanese, I would never act as you please. I would never again be a soldier. However, if I were to be reborn in this world, I wouldn't want to be a Japanese. No, I wouldn't want to be a man![47]

Other People's Property Is My Property

In this way egoism, relying solely on oneself and protecting only one's own life, has spread its roots in the minds of many Japanese who are no longer able to believe in anything.

A veteran depicted in *The Lady of Musashino* represents the way the postwar generation thinks: "In the midst of the chaos caused by defeat, he reaffirmed the belief in self-reliance that he, being a stepson, had long cultivated in his mind. Furthermore, the corruption of prisoners made him lose his confidence in man. What he saw of adult conduct in defeated Japan after being discharged from service only confirmed his conviction. He was neither interested in student movements nor did he believe in democracy."[48] There are many people, not only the youth called the *après-guerre* generation but also adults, who developed self-centeredness by letting distrust of authority grow into a distrust of the whole of mankind.

This was a result of the weakening of the concept of possession in the confusion of defeat. Especially in the army, a huge amount of government-owned war materiel was disposed of, embezzled, and

---

47. Iizuka, *Seven Years Have Passed.*
48. Ōoka Shōhei, *Musashino fujin* [The Lady of Musashino] (Tokyo: Kōdansha, 1950).

sold on the black market. "Until now, the label 'government property' on a uniform or anything else created a unique atmosphere and caused the item to be scrupulously treasured. If a man put even a scratch on it, he would be confined in a guardhouse for damaging His Majesty's property. However, the collapse of order began with an extraordinary situation wherein government property came to be at the disposal of an individual."[49] The most sacred and inviolate property of His Majesty the Emperor became private property with which people satisfied their selfish desires. It is instructive that the change in material conditions became one of the motives which stirred up the servicemen who had previously depended upon government property.

The champion of the complete egoists of the postwar generation was Yamazaki Akitsugu, whose egocentricity was born out of the confusion concerning the concept of ownership. He became the student president of the Hikari Club and later committed suicide. In his memorandum, *I Pretend to Be Evil*, he minutely describes his motivation.

> At the time of the defeat, I had been promoted to second lieutenant in the paymaster's office and was a provisions committeeman in the Asahikawa North 178th Unit. Upon the acceptance of the Potsdam Declaration, the military officers, who had always emphasized loyalty and patriotism, quoting from the Imperial Mandate and the Field Service Code, regressed to a primitive state. . . . You have to get immediate satisfaction from a girl, otherwise, someone else will get it. Go get her at once. . . . By order of Captain Sakata, I conspired with an express agent patronized by the unit in Asahikawa to conceal part of the provisions. . . . When the express agent betrayed the secret, I was apprehended on suspicion of embezzlement. . . . When I was released from prison with a sentence of a year and a half in prison and a three-year probation, Lieutenant Yokoyama, whom I had protected from accusation,

---

49. Iizuka, *Japanese Military*.

denying any relation with him, had already disposed of the concealed goods in conspiracy with the express agent. . . . Not a penny was shared with me.[50]

This experience lead Yamazaki to a philosophy of the faithlessness of man: "As human nature is originally arrogant, mean, and inconsistent, I do not trust man at all."[51] He hung a Hikari Field Service Code on the wall of the office of the Hikari Club, advocating complete egocentricity—"Let it be known that the property of others is mine; my property is mine; display a 'hikari' spirit and take away others' property"[52]—and put this philosophy into practice.

In the case of Yamazaki, egocentricity was embodied in efforts to know his own limits. That is, he attempted to find out how far he could push his self-assertion using his own ability. In this way he could be convinced of the certainty of his self. Paradoxically, he was subconsciously aware of the uncertainty of his self.

In regard to his ability, Yamazaki said, "I incorporated my speediness, youth, and intelligence in my strong enthusiasm for business. . . . I just wanted to know how far I could excel others and to realize the limits of my ability." Yet, "in my boyhood I used to ask my mother, whenever I did anything, 'Is it O.K.? Are you sure?' "[53] This is a clear example of the mental process that caused Yamazaki to become egocentric in order to cover up a weak self.

An awareness of how far he could protect himself, living with untrustworthy men, was always foremost in his mind. There were times when he hired men "only to know how far they will betray me and how well I will be able to stand against them."[54] This kind of action was motivated by a subconscious uneasiness over how much

---

50. Yamazaki Akitsugu, *Watakushi wa giakusha* [I Pretend to Be Evil] (Tokyo: Seinen Shobō, 1950).
51. Ibid.
52. Ibid.
53. Ibid.
54. Ibid.

faithlessness and despair in mankind he could bear. A magnified self-assertion is, thus, nothing but the reverse side of a lack of self-confidence.

Yamazaki, even when he talks about "an egotistic idea that the universe was born with me and will die with me," comments that "the very basis of theory is faith."[55] In brief, no matter what he claims, his theory is based on a belief in the selfishness of man and is not a result of his own deductions. Far from developing a modern self, this theory was rather a psychological support for an uncertain self.

Kotani Tsuyoshi, author of *Positive Proof* and one of the representatives of the postwar generation, often uses the term "self" in his work. He also talks about himself through the mouth of a man who begins to distrust man because of his unfortunate experience in love: "In short, I'm frustrated by women. I've learned that love is nothing but a lie. However hard you embrace each other or shed tears, both of you are after all elated by a play at identification, yet have an ultimately unchanged self. When you are driven to bay, there will remain only a plain self. And I believed in my self, feeling like nestling cheek to cheek with it. Self tries to get rid of any barrier in its way, by fair means or foul."[56]

Here, as in the case of Yamazaki, a self-centered man is visible, a man who is unable to have faith in man and who tries to get all obstacles out of the way by putting self in a high position. It is but an exaggerated self-consciousness rooted in the insecurity of an uncertain self.

Kotani confessed anxiety more honestly than Yamazaki. During an interview with Yamazaki, Kotani said, in regard to social restrictions, "As I have no confidence in my ability to break through obligation [*giri*] and sentiment [*ninjō*], I have taken a pose contrary to

---

55. Ibid.
56. Kotani Tsuyoshi, *Kakushō* [Positive Proof] (Tokyo: Kaizōsha, 1949).

them in my work."[57] Kotani realized that in order to supplement the uncertainty of his self he had to assume a pose of self-assertion. However, Yamazaki did not recognize this consciously.

Such a bluffing self-assertion needs a secure psychological base. This tendency is realized, as described later, in Yamazaki's contractualism and rationalism and Kotani's sensualism. They cling to either contract or flesh as the sole certain fact, the only positive proof, the psychological ground for upholding self.

Thus, the egocentricity of the youth of the postwar generation is a pose of the weak, negative and nonproductive in nature. Many of the crimes committed by the youth of the postwar generation and their delinquent tendencies are limited to nonproductive and pleasure-seeking activities. In this respect, they differ widely from the youth of the Meiji period.

For example, let us compare the youth of the postwar generation with Matsunaga Yasuzaemon. He was born in 1875 and became president of Tōhō Electric Power Company. He was a young man in the middle of the Meiji period, and he always thought of himself as an egocentric man because he attempted self-assertion along the lines of Fukuzawa Yukichi's "Independence and Self-Respect" taught at Keio University.

Matsunaga was filled with a positive spirit, riding on the tide of the rising capitalism of the middle Meiji period and throwing himself positively into his work. His memoirs, *A Courageous Freedom*, are worth quoting as a bold record of self-assertion rare in Japan:

> When I was young, if money were needed I earned it by doing any business except robbery and spent or saved the profit. When I was seized with sexual passion, I sneaked into the bed of another's wife. Sink or swim, leave everything to chance! After all, every matter is up to a man's courage and ability, which

---

57. Kotani Tsuyoshi, Niwa Fumio and Yamazaki Akitsugu, "Renai to jinsei to shi o kataru" ["Panel Discussion on Love, Life and Death"], *Fujinkōron* 36, no. 392 (1950).

should, in a sense, be called hormonal instinct or venturesome interest. "He advocated capitalism" or "he has become rich by exploitation"—these estimations are but labels given by others.[58]

After reading this, you may feel that his behavior is no different from that of the youth of the postwar generation. However, at the very heart of Matsunaga's self-assertion, there is no anxiety in an uncertain self; rather, his self-assertion originated from the Fuku-zawa-style self-respect. There exists a sort of intense antifeudalistic spirit. It is clearly revealed in his reminiscence of a visit to Ise Shrine early in 1897.

> After I was through with school, I became a coal dealer. When I was in business down at Yokkaichi, twenty-four or twenty-five and just a stripling, I decided to visit the Ise Shrine which people talked highly of. It was quite disgusting that what attracted my attention was only the queer scene of many pious worshippers earnestly clapping their hands and praying in silence, removing their hats and overcoats and sitting on the gravel at the foot of the stairs. While I was looking at the inside of the newly built shrine, with overcoat and hat on and with a cigar in my mouth, a guard came up to me. I was condemned for not worshipping and for smoking the cigar, which fell under some regulation of the shrine.[59]

Perhaps no other businessman under Fukuzawa's tutelage is com-parable to Matsunaga, who adopted Fukuzawa's liberalism and made known what he believed. It was a matter of course for him to harshly criticize the toadyism prevalent among the Japanese: "This national disease characterized by toadyism is epitomized in such proverbs as 'Yield to the powerful' and 'You can't win over a landlord and a crying child.' My teacher, Fukuzawa, argued severely

---

58. Matsunaga Yasuzaemon, *Yūki aru jiyū* [A Courageous Freedom] (Tokyo: Kaname Shobō, 1953).
59. Ibid.

against it in the early Meiji era. The idea of the exaltation of official life above private life and the idea of thinking of the demerits of fighting against authority just to protect oneself and one's family are derived from this racial characteristic."[60]

The self-assertion of Meiji youngsters was thus headed directly toward the development of a modern self. However, in the long run, the development of Japanese capitalism alone could not secure a bourgeois liberalism. On the contrary, inasmuch as big business joined hands with the army and government in seeking a form of protection under the state, toadyism rather than self-sufficiency has prevailed among the Japanese. Self is asserted, then, not on the basis of independent individual dignity inviolable by authority, but merely on the basis of individual greed for gain.

In the cases of Yamazaki and Kotani, as I have shown, self-assertion is carried out not as a form of resistance against authority but, in the framework of postwar society, only to satisfy their egotistic spirits. In that sense, their stand is not far from toadyism.

---

60. Ibid.

2. The Sense of Happiness

We Japanese, in contrast to foreigners, rarely use the word "happiness." Especially in daily conversation, if a person uses an expression like "I am happy," he sounds either insipid or affected. Although we write in letters phrases such as "I shall be very happy," or "I deem it a favor," these words are, after all, formal. No matter how you interpret them, they never convey true feelings.

It seems that feelings about happiness in life are for some reason diluted among the Japanese. The reason that the word "happiness" is not used daily is not only because the Japanese masses are not blessed with happiness in daily life but because they have cultivated a habit of hesitation toward happiness.

Let me trace the cause of the lack of a feeling of happiness in the Japanese. The ideas that it is dangerous to be happy, that joy is transient, and that it is a virtue to bear unhappiness have been emphasized for centuries. For the sake of convenience, I will examine these three notions individually.

Near Satisfaction Is Unsatisfactory, but Complete Satisfaction Is Hazardous

Many books on self-cultivation have been written in Japan. Almost without exception, one proverb is found in all of them: "Near satisfaction is unsatisfactory, but complete satisfaction is hazardous." To wish for complete satisfaction or to be in a state of happiness is not evil but hazardous and is considered a cause of suffering.

The philosophy of Lao-tze and Chung-tze, self-contentment

derived from minimum desire, are the source of this proverb. Lao-tze's words, "He who knows his lot is not humiliated. He who knows where to stop does not endanger himself. He will thus live longer." reveal the idea that it is hazardous to wish for more than what one is allotted.

Kamo no Chōmei said in *An Account of My Hut*, "Possessions bring many worries," and "Of all the follies of human endeavor, none is more pointless than expending treasures and spirit to build houses in so dangerous a place as the capital." He concluded, "Only in a hut built for the moment can one live without fears."[1] This, too, presents the theory that happiness is dangerous, for Chōmei sees materially favorable conditions as the source of fear and worry.

Priest Kenkō also repeatedly speaks of material happiness as being hazardous in *Essays in Idleness*. "However great his wealth may be, he is still too poor to safeguard himself, for his money is an agent which will only buy him misfortune and call in affliction. . . . No wise man ever leaves great wealth behind him when he dies. . . . There are those who will say thereafter, 'That should be mine!' and it is disgraceful to wrangle over what is left." Even giving the example of a conflict over inheritance, he asserts, "It is best to retain nothing beyond that which you really require from day to day."[2]

Chōmei and Kenkō's philosophies were merely the personal views of hermits influenced by the teachings of Lao-tze, Chung-tze, and Buddhism. These views did not appeal to the masses nor were they used as instructions for living.

However, the Tokugawa *bakufu* (military government) wished to secure a firm foundation for feudal society. It felt that it was necessary to implant a habit of simple acceptance of a rigid status system in the minds of the people in addition to control by force of arms.

Hayashi Razan, a scholar patronized by the *bakufu*, served under

---

1. Donald Keene, ed., *Anthology of Japanese Literature, from the Earliest Era to the Mid-Nineteenth Century* (New York: Grove Press, 1955), pp. 205, 198–99, 209.
2. William N. Porter, trans., *The Miscellany of a Japanese Priest* (London: Humphrey Milford, 1914), pp. 34, 112, 112–13.

four *shōgun* (generalissimos) including Tokugawa Ieyasu. He expounded the five virtues of benevolence, righteousness, propriety, knowledge, and sincerity in his *Treatise on Five Virtues*. He emphasized that happiness is hazardous: "If you indulge your desires, you will certainly ruin yourself in the future. If you give full swing to your inclinations, you will without fail destroy yourself. If you go to extremes in seeking pleasure, you will encounter sorrow in the end. If you restrict yourself, you will be able to avoid catastrophe."[3]

Not only Razan but also other Confucianists of the Tokugawa period stressed the danger in wishing for happiness in various precepts in order to prevent blasts of dissatisfaction from the masses. Kaibara Ekiken was representative of them all: "There is a limit to a man's wealth, but there is no limit to his avarice. If he indulges himself in avarice, his wealth will, without fail, be depleted. . . . If he acts as he pleases, forgetting the limit to his wealth, no matter how rich he may be he will use up all wealth. It will not only be he who suffers from impoverishment, but he becomes a nuisance to others. He will suffer all through his life and will be bad luck to his offspring."[4]

Ekiken further extends his theory: not only in wealth but in everything, to have things going well is hazardous. "Everything going quite satisfactorily with nothing more needed—this is the very source of worries. There is an old saying that *sake* should be enjoyed until one becomes slightly intoxicated and cherry blossoms should be appreciated while they are half out. This makes sense."[5]

The idea that happiness was hazardous penetrated the masses of the Tokugawa period in various highly popularized forms. It was not enough to proclaim happiness hazardous and insufficiency safer. The Way of Heaven, the superhuman and absolute power, would surely impose punishment on anyone who disagreed. For instance, if the world talked highly of a man and he was actually happy, he

---

3. Hayashi Razan, *Shunkanshō* [Treatise on Five Virtues] (1629).
4. Kaibara Ekiken, *Kadōkun* [Instructions for a Family Way of Life] (1711).
5. Kaibara Ekiken, *Yōjōkun* [Instructions for the Preservation of Health] (1713).

would surely encounter mishaps. This philosophy is stated in the proverb, "A happy event is followed by many mishaps." "In the *Book of Changes* there is a saying that the Way of Heaven will cause whatever is thriving to deteriorate. It also says that what now waxes will wane. Also, an old saying runs, 'He who stores much will lose much.' "[6] It is important to note that Heavenly punishment was not imposed only for man's avarice in not giving alms to the poor.

Another traditional Japanese idea is that if the favors rendered are too big to repay, one will ruin oneself trying to bear the burden. For example, a saying in *A Collection of Small Pebbles* reads, "If one is rendered a big favor, one's worries are big and often one ruins oneself."[7]

If happiness is seen as something given by heaven or the grace of heaven, it follows that if the grace is too great, a person will ruin himself. In other words, to be too happy is harmful; there should be a limit to a man's happiness or he will encounter mishaps. *Atsumegusa*, a text of *shingaku*, contains the saying "You must be aware that the coming of great happiness is the beginning of great misfortune."[8] This attitude seems to be a denial of happiness.

Pleasure, a condition of happiness, also incurs suffering. This is clear in *shingaku*: "Ease is the beginning of sorrow." It is also evident in the proverb "Ease is the source of pain." Kaibara said, "Worldly pleasure will turn into pain while the pleasure is still continuing. . . . It confuses one's mind, ruins one, and makes one suffer."[9]

In the Tokugawa period, some Japanese classical scholars extolled hedonism, in opposition to the idea that happiness is hazardous. But the opinion that a wish for pleasure is always accompanied by pain was deeply rooted in the Japanese. Fujitani Mitsue said, "It is a common human trait to wish for ease and hate pain. However, if you

---

6. Kaibara, *Family Way of Life*.
7. Mujū, *Shasekishū* [A Collection of Small Pebbles] (1279–1283).
8. *Atsumegusa* [Collected Papers] (1772–1788).
9. Kaibara Ekiken, *Rakukun* [Instructions for Ease] (1710).

merely hate pain, you will invite it. If you just wish for ease, you will lose it."[10]

The idea that pleasure and material happiness incur pain is still a maxim in books on self-cultivation and the art of living. "Even if you are blessed with wealth . . . you will suffer more because of that wealth. The rich do not always become happy. . . . How painful it is to hustle after money, being pressed by it, and to be busy worriedly raising funds!"[11] Nowadays the idea is not expressed in such threatening ways as "happiness is hazardous" or "he who indulges in happiness will incur the wrath of Heaven." Nevertheless, it is surprising that an attitude advocated in the times of Chōmei and Kenkō has been preserved exactly through translation into the contemporary language and is still influencing the way of life of the general population.

In postwar Japan a social psychology that creates a belief in the extreme sublimity of happiness, or hedonism, has begun to spread, in contrast to the denial of happiness. But there still exist Japanese who cannot simply accept the fact that they may be blessed by the favors of others or may come across unexpected happiness. To them favors rendered or happiness encountered by chance are accepted as a form of the aforementioned obligation, and the burden brought by the obligation is unbearable. As a result, they become frustrated by the troublesomeness and fetters attendant on happiness, instead of being content.

In *No Longer Human* Dazai Osamu vividly depicts this feeling characteristic of the Japanese, the "burden of happiness."

It was about the same time that I happened to become unexpectedly indebted to a waitress at a certain big bar in the Ginza. In spite of the fact that I met her only once, I felt constrained by the obligation, and I was worried and so afraid that I could not

---

10. Fujitani Mitsue, *Makoto ben* [A Theory of True Words] (1804–1811).

11. Ōyama Hiromichi, *Shosei hyakka jiten* [Encyclopedia for the Art of Living] (Tokyo: Saginomiya Shobō, 1951).

move an inch. . . . The night I spent with the wife of a condemned swindler was, to me, indeed a happy and liberated night. (Such a shameless word as "happy," used here without hesitation but with affirmation, will not be used again throughout the rest of my memoirs.) . . . A weak man is afraid even of happiness. He is a man who is hurt even by cotton. He is a man who is hurt even by happiness. I was irritated, confronted with the idea that I should part from her as soon as possible, before being hurt, and I laid down the smoke screen of buffoonery. . . . As days went by after parting from her, my feeling of joy faded away and, contrarily, I was afraid of being indebted over a slight obligation and felt heavily constrained.[12]

The philosophy that happiness makes it necessary to shoulder a burden seems to have some relationship to the old idea that happiness is hazardous. This is especially true of the idea that a big favor is a hazard, as can be seen in *A Collection of Small Pebbles*.

Nothing Can Be Carried with You into Death

Another philosophy which denies happiness in this world is a Japanese nihilism that stresses the transiency of happiness. It is derived from the notion of impermanency salient in Buddhism, long the underlying philosophy of Japanese life.

Typical examples of this way of thinking can be found in *Essays in Idleness* and *An Account of My Hut*. Kenkō and Chōmei, however, differ in many respects in their understanding of the notion of impermanency.

Kenkō professes that since the present life is temporary and transient, it is not worth clinging to. Even in a mansion, "well, indeed, none can live forever, and a single glance tells me that all this will

---

12. Dazai Osamu, *Ningen shikkaku* [No Longer Human] (Tokyo: Chikuma Shobō, 1948).

pass away like a puff of smoke." Because "from all this we may learn how vain it is to make plans for the unknown future," we know that both our present life and our fame among posterity is all in vain and not worth seeking after. Herein the idea of reclusion is brought forth: "The truth is, if a man is really convinced that the world is but transient and honestly wishes to be rid of this fleeting existence, how can he take pleasure in serving his lord day and night, or be fearless in caring for his family? The heart distracted by worldly ties is liable to change, and it is hard therefore to follow the Way without the tranquility of solitude. . . . As we are born human beings, we should in return at any cost shun worldly desires."[13]

Chomei, in *An Account of My Hut*, also emphasized that happiness in this world is ephemeral and unworthy of trust. "For whose benefit does he torment himself in building houses that last but a moment, for what reason is his eye delighted by them? This too we do not know. Which will be first to go, the master or his dwelling? One might just as well ask this of the dew on the morning-glory."[14] In other words, no matter how you extol happiness and pleasure, they are hollow.

Japanese junior high school students learn such passages and are taught that this way of thinking represents the Japanese philosophy of life. Moreover, in Japanese literary thought there exists the didactic view that literature should be used to implant the notion of impermanency in people's minds.

The medieval poets Shinkei and Sōgi are good examples of this didacticism. They contended that *renga* (linked verse) should be composed to emphasize impermanency and make people aware of transiency. Shinkei says in *Whispering*, "The purpose of *renga* is the description of transiency and the expression of the pathos of life and nature. It is meant to soften the minds of barbarians or fierce warriors

---

13. Porter, *Miscellany*, pp. 16, 28, 50–51.
14. Keene, *Anthology*, p. 198.

and to encourage them to become aware of the principle of a transient world."[15]

Poetry is thus a means for awakening readers to the transiency and ephemerality of life. Sentimental poetry characteristic of the Japanese, which attempts to find the transiency of man in nature, has been transmitted from the medieval *renga* to current popular songs.

During the Tokugawa period, the notion of impermanency penetrated the philosophy of life of the masses through easily understood sermons. For example, passages from a famous poem of the Zen monk Hakuin read: "Even a millionaire has nothing to possess when he dies. . . . Life is evanescent, so it is called the life of dew. . . . Then in such an unreliable world as this, should you still want to save gold and silver?"[16]

As a monk, Hakuin taught the uselessness of "unreliable" worldly happiness to the masses; however, the notion of impermanency emerges even in the work of Saikaku, who often thought practically. He also expressed the uselessness after death of happiness gained through money, saying, "The floating world is a phantasm. It is a momentary smoke. What then will one be after death? Gold and silver are more worthless than tiles and pebbles and are useless for the journey to the nether world."[17]

Even Shiba Kōkan, who was one of the few rationalists to appear in the Tokugawa period, wrote a similar reflection on his past life in an essay of his later years, *Scribbles of Shunpa-rō*.

> While living in this world from my youth to my old age,
>   I have felt that life is indeed frivolous.
> The world is nothing but a fuss
>   In a temporary abode in a street;

---

15. Shinkei, *Sasamegoto* [Whispering] (1463).
16. Hakuin, *Zen aku tanemaki kagami wasan* [Buddhist Hymn Mirroring the Sowing of Good and Evil] (1835).
17. Ihara Saikaku, *Nihon eitaigura* [The Eternal Storehouse of Japan] (1688).

No one remains
In twilight skies.[18]

The notion of impermanency was highly esteemed among warriors as the basis for a disregard for death and restraint from avarice. The notion of impermanency for warriors is explained in *Basic Principles of the Way of the Warrior*: "The primary purpose of the warrior is to be ready to die day or night. . . . He should be prepared to have his life be a reality today but not tomorrow." If, on the contrary, "he looks upon death from a distance, since he expects to live long in this world, he will eventually have many wishes, become greedy, want to acquire others' possessions, become stingy, and come to possess the state of mind of a townsman or peasant." Inasmuch as a true warrior "considers this world frivolous, his greed eventually fades away . . . and even his nature grows refined."[19] In other words, to know the ephemerality of life is, to a warrior, the basis for the refinement of his personality. As mentioned earlier, to look upon death from a distance means to cling to life and to be mundane; therefore, warriors were always urged to be conscious of impermanency.

An essay written during the Tenpō period, which lasted from 1830 to 1844, deplores the state of mind of warriors who neglect to think of impermanency: "With a limited life, they are blinded by endless avarice, neglecting to ponder over impermanency to the slightest degree, being thirsty only for mundane objects, and going on like this for a thousand years; it is indeed shameful."[20]

A negative sense of impermanency, bearing no resemblance to chivalrous loyalty and courage, was firmly implanted in the warrior's mind. This negative sense of impermanency must have served as a relief from the irrationality perceptible in a warrior's

---

18. Shiba Kōkan, *Shunpa-rō hikki* [Scribbles of Shunpa-rō] (1811).
19. Daidōji Yūzan, *Budō shoshinshū* [Basic Principles of the Way of the Warrior] (1834).
20. Shiga Shinobu, *Risai zuihitsu* [Risai's Essay] (1838).

service or death in battle. When the spirit of the way of the warrior is thus observed from the angle of latent weakness and resignation, it seems somehow pitiful.

A Zen monk, Suzuki Shōsan, who was of warrior origin, cited the "mind to perceive illusory transformation and impermanency" as one of the significant frames of mind of the warrior. He said that if a warrior could "liberate himself from numerous attachments," his "suffering and agony would be reduced even when he dies in battle."[21]

It was important to both warriors and townsmen to take the existing world lightly in the face of impermanency. In *Praise with Limited Words* subservience and resignation rooted in a sense of impermanency, a denial of happiness, are well delineated: "You ought to take the existing world as an overnight lodging, an illusory world. ... If you could think thus, you would be able to bear the unbearable and would be courageous enough to fulfill your duties for the sake of the life to come. Never think that life is long. If you take that attitude, things in this life will become important, and you will begin to lead a life of immorality."[22]

A man could hardly bear the thought of considering this world impermanent unless he were a Buddhist who could believe in the next world or a warrior who had a firm determination to sacrifice his life for the sake of his lord. Relief from the notion of impermanency depended upon the availability of concepts of the absolute and permanent such as the life to come and loyalty, in contrast to the impermanency of this world.

Thus the Japanese sense of impermanency is characterized by a belief in the existence of an absolute being hidden behind the denial of happiness in this world. Hence, it differs substantially from western nihilism, which rejects any absolute being, and should be distinguished as the Japanese version of nihilism.

---

21. Suzuki Shōsan, *Banmin tokuyō* [Moral Lesson for Millions] (1631).
22. *Ichigon hōdan* [Praise with Limited Words] (1648).

This Japanese nihilism has survived in the minds of the Japanese. In 1926, the beginning of the Shōwa period, a nationalist at the court spoke reminiscently about the relationship between the notion of impermanency and emperor worship. "The performance of human strength is, even at its best, frail and ephemeral. . . . Therefore, all living beings were equally aware of the impermanency and ephemerality of man's life, and they always looked for a being not subject to change. . . . What mankind was searching for was our divine land, Japan, and a personal god, the Emperor."[23] His words clearly reveal the fact that the psychological tradition of Japanese nihilism, at least its search for permanency behind obvious impermanency, was easily connected with the logic and psychology of fascism, resting upon an absolute being in the figure of the Emperor.

Despite differences in their situations, feelings arising from Japanese nihilism, in which the sense of impermanency and the sense of the absolute are intermingled, are found in the notes of students who died in battle as members of suicide units. "I shall die to become a cloud in the sky. I don't know when it will be. Inevitability is the way of this world."[24] "We are birds traveling with no destination. To us fliers, today's meeting is tomorrow's parting. I am resolved to offer my indeterminable life for the sake of the Emperor and for the sake of my country."[25]

The youth of the suicide units seem also to have wished to live with an absolute being called Perpetual Justice, heedful of impermanency and renouncing this world like *samurai*. The normal wish of a young man for a long life was obliterated by Japanese nihilism.

The notion of impermanency is, however, not only connected with the problem of death. Today people still feel that it is signifi-

23. Kageyama Masaharu, *7.5 Jiken kōhan kiroku* [Records of the Trials of the July 5th Incident] (Tokyo: Daitōjuku Shuppanbu, 1942).

24. Committee for Compiling Notes of Student Soldiers Killed in World War II, eds., *Haruka naru yamakawani* [To Far-off Mountains and Rivers] (Tokyo: Mikasa Shobō, 1952).

25. Ibid.

cant to be aware of impermanency. It is, first of all, this awareness which helps a person remain calm and unruffled in unexpected misfortune. It is, so to speak, the cultivation of the notion of impermanency as a means to a negative psychological immunity from misfortune. It is similar to the attitude of the warrior or military man toward death, which is even today expounded as a fitting attitude for daily life for the Japanese. A prewar book on self-cultivation reads: "What attitude should we always assume, since life is so impermanent? What frame of mind should we assume when we are confronted with impermanency? This is the way to live cheerfully and, at the same time, to turn misfortune into a blessing."[26]

The tea cult, which is still considered by many Japanese to be a fitting means of special self-cultivation, preserves the idea that its purpose is to create awareness of the sense of impermanency and readiness for any misfortune encountered in life. A tea ceremony is called *ichigo ichie*, a meeting once in a lifetime. All who share in the same tea ceremony should take it as a once-in-a-lifetime opportunity, acting as if they would never see one another again. It is said that the sense of impermanency felt in a tea ceremony lies in this attitude. "A tea ceremony occurs once in a lifetime . . . its participants never see one another again. . . . It is of no duration, fading vainly like a dream . . . which shows the ephemerality of life. . . . Truly, this is what it is."[27]

It is not known how many people consider a tea ceremony in this way; however, the incorporation of the sense of impermanency in the tea cult, which is merely a cultivated taste, is characteristic of the Japanese life of refinement. Paradoxically, the sense of impermanency in the tea cult appears to be experienced merely as a hobby and as a spiritual extravagance by those who lead a life of comparative material ease.

---

26. Tamura Reishō, *Omakase to jinsei* [Passivity and Life] (Tokyo: Tenshindō-honbu, 1942).
27. Tanaka Kishirō, *Nihon chadō ron* [On the Tea Ceremony in Japan] (Tokyo: Jūjiya Shoten, 1940).

In contrast to the psychological immunity from misfortune provided by a belief in impermanency, there emerges an attitude of active anticipation of unexpected happiness arising out of the impermanency of life. In this respect, the sense of impermanency comes not only to be connected with the denial of happiness but with the denial of misfortune. The sense of impermanency, as I will show in the chapter on fatalism, is connected with the spirit of gambling, and it develops into the fatalism characteristic of the Japanese.

A book on self-cultivation, for example, which adopted numerous components of Buddhism, explains the connection between the sense of impermanency and the anticipation of happiness in this way: "Common people . . . go through hardships; therefore, existing in a state of impermanency is at least a comfort to them, and they live with a hope for tomorrow's prosperity. . . . Because we are in a state of impermanency, we can hope to enjoy tomorrow's prosperity."[28]

The sense of impermanency provides both immunity from misfortune and anticipation of happiness; these are the two faces of Japanese nihilism. In a slightly different form, a sense of impermanency resembling western nihilism has been introduced to modern Japan. The sense of impermanency of Japanese nihilism is, so to speak, realistic, for it is related to the problem of happiness. Modern western nihilism, however, does not bother with happiness or unhappiness but contains a sense of absolute impermanency that denies the realities of life.

The modern sense of impermanency is often expressed in contemporary literature. Apart from the joy of happiness and the sorrow of unhappiness, there is a feeling that only a spirit desperate in its search for reality in actual life comes to find it.

Inasmuch as Nagai Kafū has educated himself in modern European culture, his sense of impermanency differs from that of Japanese nihilism, and he often has the characters in his work talk about a

28. Tomomatsu Entai, *Mukuyuru kokoro* [A Grateful Mind] (Tokyo: Jitsugyō no Nihonsha, 1941).

state of mind derived from absolute nihilism. An Asakusa musician who appears in *The Dancing Girl* speaks reminiscently: "It has already been ten years since I became a violinist in Rokku [an amusement area]. I feel that my life, which has been dissolute and wild, seems to be coming to an end. It's a feeling somewhat sorrowful yet desirable, deep and sad."[29]

The author's sense of impermanency is depicted in *A Strange Tale from East of the River* when he became intimate with Oyuki, a prostitute living in a back street. He parted from her—"neither Oyuki nor I knew the other's name or home"—and looked back at the relationship with nostalgia, for "once we parted, there was neither chance nor means to bring us together again."[30] This sense of impermanency is also clearly revealed in the deep emotion of Dr. Matsuzaki depicted in *Before and After the Rainy Season*: "I have come to feel as if there existed neither past nor future but only daily joys and sorrows in human life. Neither praise nor censure seems worth my consideration."[31]

Herein the sense of impermanency can be found in the joy and sorrow of daily living. But the next words of the old scholar show that the modern sense of impermanency rests upon something like an awakening rooted in Japanese nihilism: " 'If it were so, I would say that my life was the happiest life of all. I'm sixty but have not yet had illness, and I have no shame in playing with a twenty-year-old waitress, regardless of those present, often feeling as if I were a youth. Looking at it from this point only, my fortune is far better than a king's.' And Dr. Matsuzaki was about to laugh in spite of himself."[32]

Within the sense of impermanency there still remains composure

29. Nagai Kafū, "Odoriko" ["The Dancing Girl"], *Tembō* (1946).
30. Nagai Kafū, *Bokutō kidan* [A Strange Tale from East of the River] (Tokyo: Asahi Shimbun Sha, 1937).
31. Nagai Kafū, *Tsuyu no atosaki* [Before and after the Rainy Season] (Tokyo: Chūō Kōron Sha, 1931).
32. Ibid.

enough to laugh and deliverance from a deep concern for praise and censure as a result of his having a "Japanese" or Zen-like feeling of accommodating himself to nature. Therefore, Kafū's sense of impermanency is not a hindrance to his living but is, on the contrary, a relief to him. Kafū has neither gone insane nor killed himself.

The impermanency felt by the generation after Kafū, however, drove them to impatience and despair and wouldn't let them stay in one place, in happiness or unhappiness.

The novelist depicted in Oda Sakunosuke's *A Phase of Life* expresses a sense of impermanency different from Kafū's. Despite the superficial resemblance, the novelist found no relief in his feeling. "But we can 'follow neither the leftists nor rightists, showing distrust in thought and system,' but live the springtime of life 'not falling into an extremely uneasy condition, yet with an ambiguous look—whether awakened or not awakened, young or old,'—explaining, 'It's a kind of decadence.' "[33]

In brief, neither Oda nor the succeeding generation could find spiritual stability, and they ended up with the modern sense of impermanency, which sees only agitation and change as constant. Therefore, to Oda, "only at the moment when I depicted my wandering self lying idly at an inn, did my writing become refreshed. A kaleidoscopic change in time and place was the sole aim of the fool who attempted to protect his sensibility, which had neither system nor thought, from injury caused by letting it submerge in only one spot."[34]

A distillation of the modern sense of impermanency leaves only despair, insanity, and suicide. Dazai Osamu in *No Longer Human* could not help saying, "I have no feeling of happiness or unhappiness now. Everything only passes away. In the so-called human world where I have agonizingly lived, this was the only thing that seemed to be *real*."[35]

---

33. Oda Sakunosuke, *Sesō* [A Phase of Life] (Tokyo: Chūō Kōron Sha, 1948).
34. Ibid.
35. Dazai, *No Longer Human*; Dazai's italics.

3. The Sense of Unhappiness

Just as the sense of happiness of the Japanese tends to be twisted into a Japanese nihilism, a view of unhappiness or hardship that is unique to the Japanese has become a sort of psychological tradition.

As I have mentioned before, although the Japanese have not grown accustomed to using the word "happiness," they have a rich vocabulary for expressing its absence: "unhappiness," "hardship," and "difficulty," and modifiers such as "sorrowful," "pitiful," and "lonely." When the words used in Japanese popular songs are analyzed, the most frequently used common noun, even in the postwar present, is "tears." "Cry," the verb form, and "sorrowful," "distressing," "dear," and "lonesome," the adjectival forms, are, except for "lovely," the words most frequently used. And the word "lovely" is not necessarily used in happy songs. Popular songs, appealing to the taste of Japan's masses, in many cases express a state of unhappiness rather than happiness.

Viewed from this angle, it is obvious that the Japanese are always followed by unhappiness and have many chances to think about it in relation to their own lives as well as in connection with psychology. Let me, then, suggest a psychology which might be called the sense of unhappiness, in contrast to the Japanese sense of happiness.

First, the Japanese have discovered a means of easing complaints or dissatisfaction by resigning themselves to a situation. Japanese books on self-cultivation, which give psychological solutions for dissatisfaction, are unique. It is not an overstatement to say that this resignation is the core of Japanese self-cultivation.

Secondly, in Japan, there exists a state of mind which can be called "insufficiency-ism" or "imperfectionism," the belief that unhappiness and misfortune are not to be negatively endured or diverted but are rather to be positively accepted. Unhappiness and misfortune are seen as desirable for self-cultivation; suffering is seen as concomitant with repaying a favor rendered, a type of service; and insufficiency or imperfection is viewed as desirable and attractive. This attitude is close to masochism.

There are four solutions generally suggested for unhappiness: to bear one's present situation as it is, to find some reason to abide by the inevitable, to calm oneself by finding some diversion, and to blame oneself and reproach or punish oneself as a result.

True Patience Lies in Bearing the Unbearable

The quickest way to attain enlightenment in an unfortunate situation is to endure it without uttering a word of complaint. No matter how bitterly one is treated, one should bear it.

For centuries in Japan, rulers have forced this endurance upon the ruled as the highest virtue. Don't argue; just be patient with your situation, taking it as a direct order. Kaibara Ekiken was an authority on endurance:

> There is much to be endured. All results from anger and avarice. To submit yourself to poverty and make nothing of it is to subdue your avarice. To take the heartlessness and impoliteness of others toward you as the natural behavior of ordinary men, holding no anger or grudge, is to endure anger. If you could subdue all your anger and avarice, you would be peaceful at heart, feel at ease, have no worries, give no trouble to others, have no shame, have no suffering, have no anxiety about your future, and have no misfortunes. . . . The reason for endurance is that it is quite beneficial for living at ease.[1]

---

1. Kaibara Ekiken, *Rakukun* [Instructions for Ease] (1710).

Ekiken called this book on self-cultivation, in which the spirit of endurance is expounded, *Instructions for Ease*. What, then, ought one to do to attain a state of ease, where no matter how severely one is treated one feels that human beings in general are like that and one bears with them without anger? Answers to this question are never given. In any event, you should be patient, and then you will be blessed with something good. This is a mere statement of consequences, and no reasons are given.

A Buddhist hymn of the Zen monk Hakuin reads, "This world of ours is but a world of endurance and nothing turns out as we wish."[2] Accordingly, to build up the habit of submission to any treatment is to create the habit of endurance which eventually leads one to a peaceful and tranquil state of mind. It is, in any event, an unconditional resignation with no reason, a spiritlessness.

Unconditional resignation, as I have mentioned before, can hardly be obtained unless one is placed by force under absolute submission to authority for a long period of time. Military education is an example: "A new recruit gets scolded, whatever he does. In the course of time, he becomes indifferent and immune to scolding. When resignation to the situation as one in which scolding is inevitable is embedded in him, he can generally accustom himself to military life."[3]

The discipline of resignation derived from the teaching of the *Hagakure*, the endurance of daily bitterness by taking it as a day's bitterness, has been preserved until the present day. "If you could think that service is but today's service, you could do anything. Only one day's service, no matter what it may be, is bearable. The following day is the same."[4] By living daily with the proverb, "True

---

2. Hakuin, *Zen aku tanemaki kagami wasan* [Buddhist Hymn Mirroring the Sowing of Good and Evil] (1835).

3. Iizuka Kōji, *Nihon no guntai* [The Japanese Military] (Tokyo: Tokyo Daigaku Shuppanbu, 1950).

4. Yamamoto Jinemon Jōchō, *Hagakure* [In the Shade of Leaves] (1716).

patience lies in bearing what is unbearable," one may attain the state of resignation.

Hardships Always Follow Man

However, it is not so simple for a man to be tolerant of his unfortunate lot, putting logic aside. Therefore, resignation must be rationalized.

First, there is fatalism. This is the idea of attributing everything to fate, saying that the happiness or unhappiness of man has been predestined in his previous life or is the retribution of his karma. This will be explained in detail later as a peculiar aspect of Japanese fatalism.

Secondly, the idea that life is spent in the world of endurance, primarily a world of suffering, is tendered. This idea is expounded mainly in Buddhism, where life is seen merely as a place of karmic suffering. Buddhism finds suffering in everything. In each individual being, there are four sufferings, birth, age, disease, and death; in human relations, parting with what we love, meeting with what we hate, unattained aims, and all the ills of the five *skandhas* (components of an intelligent being) are found.

Education based on the perception of life in a world of suffering was encouraged around 1935 in the writings of the disseminators of Buddhism. Tomomatsu Entai, who was representative of these writers, said, "A human being is originally suffering. It is, therefore, prideful to think you can get along in the world without hardship."[5]

It is obvious in the following words of a Buddhist that a pessimistic view of life, in which one is resolved that life is karmic suffering, becomes the psychological basis of resignation: "Because one's view of life is pessimistic, there arises a sense of resignation which gives

---

5. Tomomatsu Entai, *Mukuyuru kokoro* [A Grateful Mind] (Tokyo: Jistsugyō no Nihonsha, 1941).

peace to society and helps a wife bear the cruel treatment of her mother-in-law."[6] Ichihashi, the speaker of these words, seems to be a big businessman, but I doubt whether, with such an utterly pessimistic view of life, he can run a business. In any event, he is not aware that his view is used as an excuse to make people unconditionally submissive. He also said, "A pessimistic view of life teaches you endurance and brings forth a sense of duty."[7] This is an utterly Japanese view adopted as a psychological support of the sense of duty. Duty is not seen in opposition to rights but is part of the suffering of life. This comes to be related to the question of *giri* (obligation), which I will deal with later. This attitude is one of the obvious characteristics of Japanese social psychology.

To live in the world of suffering is to live as if one were serving an indefinite prison term. Once a man has made such a resolution, he is able to reconcile himself to unhappiness. This attitude can be quite effective as a means to achieve immunity from unhappiness.

However, for those who are unable to agree on such a mundane example as karmic suffering, immunity from unhappiness is preached in more profound words and expressions. Tomomatsu uses such terms as "nothingness" and "void": "The Japanese people take note of 'nothingness.' They contemplate 'void.' If the worst should happen, they are in readiness to strip themselves bare. They are resolved that 'nothingness' is the primary state. . . . They are from the beginning prepared for being placed in the very depths. They are ready for the worst."[8]

The resignation mentioned in this quote is neither despair nor disappointment but rather an attitude of constant anticipation of the worst. Therefore, if something should happen, one would not attempt every possible means to get over the loss; on the contrary, as

---

6. Ichihashi Zennosuke, *Ninku to jihi to teinen* [Endurance, Mercy, and Perception of Reason] (Osaka: Katsuragi Shoten, 1944).

7. Ibid.

8. Tomomatsu, *A Grateful Mind.*

he has constantly anticipated that it could be so, he would not be flurried. This is the Japanese resignation. It is not giving up, saying, "You've got me," but rather a constant resignation.

If this attitude is intensified, it becomes what the *Hagakure* calls *hisshi no kannen*, a sense of inevitable death: "Calm your mind every morning, be resolved to meet the moment when you may be mangled by arrows, guns, spears, and swords, swept away by billows, cast into a fire, struck by thunderbolts, and drawn into an earthquake, fall over a serveral-thousand-foot precipice, die of illness or a sudden death, and die earnestly every morning in your mind." "Out from the eaves one is amid the dead and outside the gate the enemy is seen" means "not to be cautious but to die beforehand."[9]

If this is so, *hisshi* means not to strive at the risk of one's life but to always expect and be reconciled beforehand to the worst, death. If one could constantly make sure of psychological immunity to death by imagining every possible case of violent death, one would not play the coward. It is, therefore, neither precaution nor a cautious mind but a more passive frame of mind. Herein the evanescence and frailty of the way of the warrior are again manifested.

Contrary to the spirit of the *Hagakure*, in a more popularized art of self-cultivation, a song quoted in *Tōkyū-jutsu* expresses the resignation of the Japanese well: "When cherry blossoms bloom, they are foreordained to fall; when one gets drunk on *sake*, he is doomed to become sober; when two meet, they end with parting. Cherry blossoms, do not burst so fully into bloom, for you are soon destined to fall."

Even now, for the majority of the Japanese resignation is a firm prop in living a life full of hardships. This is certainly evidence that since the Tokugawa period, when *shingaku* taught that hardship was the shadow of man, that his duty was to undergo hardship, and that hate it as he might, it would never leave him, the life of the masses has not improved noticeably.

---

9. Yamamoto, *Shade of Leaves.*

Know Your Lot

For generations, resignation has been taught in the form of such maxims as "Know your own lot" and "Cut your coat according to your cloth," which are based on ideas of *bungen*, one's place in life and *bunzai*, one's status in life. A phrase in Confucian teaching, *chisoku anbun*, "know how to be satisfied with your portion in life," was frequently suggested as a means to a successful life during the Tokugawa period and is still considered to be a desirable attitude for living.

A similar attitude is eulogized in the Buddhist hymn of Hakuin, to whom I have already referred. However, his view is quite unusual because in it the discontent and dissatisfaction of the poor are acknowledged: "Bear the teaching of the Buddha in mind. Avarice is endless. The more one has avarice, the more one is discontented. Learn how to be satisfied. It is natural to struggle with poverty, but despicable is he who has property and yet struggles."[10]

A view like Hakuin's seems to have been exceptional. In the Tokugawa status society "learn how to be satisfied" tied to "one's portion in life" was an expediency for cultivating a submissive attitude toward one's superior and contentment with one's lot. Typical examples are the sayings in the *Instructions for Ease* by Kaibara Ekiken: "Wealth and nobility, poverty and humility, all has not resulted from one's wisdom or folly but from one's innate lot." Therefore, "be contented with your lot and do not be envious or wish for something beyond your reach. . . . Don't have a grudge against Heaven or blame others."[11]

Learning how to be satisfied is, even at the present, highly recommended as one of the secrets of a successful life. For instance, the *Encyclopedia for the Art of Living* says, "You have a tree that bears

---

10. Hakuin, *Buddhist Hymn Mirroring the Sowing of Good and Evil.*
11. Kaibara, *Instructions for Ease.*

money. Don't you know that? It is your attitude. Learn how to be contented. No matter how rich you are, you are as good as poor unless you are satisfied. However poor you are, you are as good as rich when you are satisfied."[12]

Life Is like the Moon Covered by a Cloud and Flowers Scattered by the Wind

Along with *chisoku anbun* thought, in which a person's position is considered in terms of human society, as in *mibun* (social status) and *bunzai* (status in life), there is also the view which considers each individual's position in nature or the universe.

Thus, the concept of lot has two aspects, that laid down by *tendō* (the Way of Heaven) and *tenmei* (the mandate of Heaven), and that destined to man as part of the natural phenomena. The words of Kyūō, a *shingaku* scholar, explain *chisoku anbun* in terms of man's lot in nature: "Trees and grass bear fruits and flowers; this is identical with the prosperity of man. As the trees and grass on which flowers blossom and fruits ripen are different in size, men also differ in wealth and poverty, distress and fame."[13]

Man, because of his willfulness against nature, is unable to become happy. "Your lack of prosperity is ascribable to your constant indulgence in self-partiality and willfulness."[14] Ebara Koyata, a commentator on the Buddhist view of life, says something similar: "Even the phenomenon of life, in fact, exists where it should be, in accordance with its lot. . . . The phenomenon of life is, after all, one of the natural phenomena."[15]

---

12. Ōyama Hiromichi, *Shosei hyakka jiten* [Encyclopedia for the Art of Living] (Tokyo: Saginomiya Shobō, 1951).

13. Kyūō, *Kyūō dōwa* [Kyūō's Moral Discourses] (1834).

14. Ibid.

15. Ebara Koyata, *Kokoro no okidokoro* [The Place Where Your Mind Should Be] (Tokyo: Kōfūkan, 1951).

The Buddhist concept of the unity of nature and man has permeated Japanese thought. When asked about his view of life, Takahama
Kyoshi, a *haiku* poet, said, "Nature is an essential force which actuates
every entity, including every social phenomenon. . . . Man's life
coincides with the movements of nature and heavenly bodies, as
flowers bloom and leaves scatter. It is animated along with cosmic
phenomena and is annihilated with them."[16]

This is only one example. The Japanese have been close to nature
for centuries. They seem to have had more interest in nature than in
society, and they have made great use of natural symbols in literature
and the visual arts. What is the reason for this preoccupation? At
least one of the reasons seems to have been the perception of nature
and life as one and the same, and the ascription of unhappiness and
misfortune to the transciency and evanescence of nature and things
impermanent.

Many attribute the fondness of the Japanese for making nature the
theme of literary works to the scenic beauty of Japan. However, it
should not only be ascribed to the fact that fine scenic views and the
beauty in the changes of the seasons are likely objects for literary
works, but to a traditional attitude of looking upon nature in per-
sonification and, in reverse, upon man in naturalization.

This attitude is most clearly observable in the *renga* (linked verse)
of medieval times. The *renga*, according to Shinkei and Sōgi, reveals
things common to nature and life through form and content. In
Tsukuba Dialogue Nijō Yoshimoto stated that the format of the *renga*
mirrors the impermanency and vagaries of nature and life. "In the
renga, a feeling is not linked with its succeeding feeling. The phases
of prosperity and decline, distress and joy undergoing continuous
change are not different from the phases of the world. Isn't the idea
of the falling of blossoms and leaves reflected in yesterday becoming

---

16. Takahama Kyoshi in *Watakushi no tetsugaku* [My Philosophy], Committee for
the Study of the Science of Thought, eds. (Tokyo: Chūō Kōron Sha, 1950).

today, spring shifting into autumn, and cherry blossoms giving way to autumn leaves?"[17]

Sōgi firmly maintained that poetry was training in finding the evanescence of life and the changeableness of nature: "The art of poetry is to bear in mind only mercy. If you speculated upon the reason for life and death, even in the falling of blossoms and leaves, you could soften the demon in your heart and would arrive at the reason for enlightenment and the ultimate reality."[18] "Even observing the falling of blossoms and leaves, who could avoid the implications and rest upon the idea of permanency?"[19]

Shinkei, prior to Sōgi, defined the art of poetry as that which "infuses the idea of the evanescence of life."[20] He said, "When you see the falling blossoms and leaves or the dew on the grass, you must realize that this world is dreamlike and illusory."[21] Both seem to describe a similar frame of mind.

Shinkei deplored the fact that those who "are audacious and covetous . . . play with words, using such terms as 'unhappy,' 'painful,' 'sorrowful,' 'dreary,' 'weary of life,' and 'self-effacing,' but to me they are ridiculous."[22] He felt, conversely, that the art of poetry was a form of self-cultivation meant to reform an audacious and covetous attitude. He seems to have regarded the art of poetry as a spiritual tool to help a person see the impermanency in nature, become resigned to man's misfortune, and attain enlightenment.

The identification of nature with life found in *renga* can be seen today in the popular *rōkyoku* chants.

> Knowing the destiny of flowers,
> A sevenfold and seven-colored rainbow of love,

---

17. Nijō Yoshimoto, *Tsukuba mondō* [Tsukuba Dialogue] (1357–1372).
18. Sōgi, *Azuma mondō* [Azuma Dialogue] (1467 or 1470).
19. Sōgi, *Kokin jikkōshō* [Discourses on the *Kokinshū*] (1501).
20. Shinkei, *Sasamegoto* [Whispering] (1463).
21. Kensai, *Shinkei sōzu teikin* [Precepts of the Monk Shinkei] (1488).
22. Ibid.

A straightforward mind to bloom into love . . .
Standing along the shore of a mountain lake,
I have pity on the destiny of the flowers.
      "Seven-colored Flowers"

Grass lasts only one autumn;
Man lives only one life;
Do I care how short my life is?
      "Yataro, the Traveling Hat"

At the port where I parted from you
   leaving my heart behind,
A sea gull flies all alone
   in the rain.
Ah, like a scarlet camellia,
   like a scarlet camellia falling to the ground,
Why am I weeping, tonight too,
   at an empty dream,
Our love at the spa?
      Saijō Yaso, "A Port of Scarlet Camellias"

Examples like these can be given in large numbers. It is obvious
that the contemporary popular songs are related to the sense of impermanency in the medieval *renga*. Both see the disappointment of
love in the falling of blossoms and leaves.

The shadow of the moon is subject to waxing and waning.
Yesterday's pool is today's shallows.
It is inevitable,
   for human life is doomed to change.
But how pitiful is Kunisada Chūji,
   who would be at the zenith of power.
      "Akagi Lullaby"

Like a cloud to the moon
   and a storm to the flowers,

Indeed, the floating world
is beyond our sway.
"A *Yakuza* with a *Samisen*"

Like a cloud to the moon
and the wind to the flowers,
How uncertain
human destiny is!
After all, it is tossed about and swept away
by the raging waves
of the floating world.
There is no way to ease the grief.
"Akagi Nocturne"

Unhappiness in life is expressed through the guise of nature; because of the evanescence of nature, man should realize that it is senseless to grieve and should become reconciled to fate. This view of nature as a means of resignation to unhappiness stems from a psychological tradition unique to the Japanese.

Life Is a Journey in the Floating World

Together with the identification of nature with life, the Japanese have used the convention of comparing life to a journey. The phrases "a travel through life" or "journey in the world" are typical examples. Numerous literary works attempt to depict the evanescence and frailty of life or to show flowing and changing using the travel convention. A journey, symbolizing life, and the traveler's loneliness, symbolizing unhappiness in life, are often employed in poetry and stories.

A critique of medieval poetry explaining how to achieve the correct mental attitude for composing poetry stressed that if one would recite a Chinese poem depicting the lonely state of a traveler, one could compose a fine and touching poem. A passage in *Shōtetsu's*

Talks reads: "Teika said, 'When you are composing a *waka* poem, if you would recite a poem from *A Collection of Po Chü-i's Poems*— "Thinking of mother in the old home town, My tears in the autumn wind; In the inn, none but my roaming heart in the evening rain"— your mind would be uplifted, and you could compose a fine poem.' "23

Japanese sentimentalism, in which the sadness of a journey and the evanescence of life are blended, is one of the elements which appeals to the masses in present-day popular songs and *rōkyoku* chants. The following popular songs are representative of this type:

> My wandering self, at any rate,
>> must come to a weather-beaten end.
>>> Saijō Yaso, "A Wandering Guitar"

> I'm a wandering singer.
>> Yesterday I was in the east
>> and today in the west.
>>> "The Tears of a Mother and Child Crane"

> A circus girl
>> On an endless journey,
> Let me cry for tomorrow
>> in the shade of a *nobori* flag.
>>> Saijō Yaso, "I'm a Sad Tiny Pigeon"

> When a light rain falls,
>> even my heart becomes wet.
> My heart in travel is
>> dreary somehow.
>>> Saijō Yaso, "A Port of Scarlet Camellias"

Roaming in travels and parting in sorrow are conceived as certain phases of the floating world, and life is called "a journey in the float-

---

23. Shōtetsu, *Shōtetsu monogatari* [Shōtetsu's Talks] (1430).

ing world." A passage of a *rōkyoku* chant reveals this attitude, in which roaming is perceived as one of the vicissitudes of life:

> I don't care which way I head
>   on a journey in the floating world.
> It's all up to the wind.
>   "A *Yakuza* with a *Samisen*"

Oda Sakunosuke, in *A Phase of Life*, delineates this state of mind vividly: "Since I was brought up as a vagrant, I have painted all my work, from the time of my first work, in only one color, wandering. To me, life, when I think of it, is flowing and changing. . . . Only when I depicted my wandering self lying idly at an inn did my writing become refreshed."[24]

The fact that there have been many Japanese literary works with journey themes means not only that people go on a journey because of fine scenic views, from which descriptions of scenery can be created, but that the convention of the journey of life has permeated the minds of the Japanese.

Take Pleasure in the Moon, Snow, and Flowers

A psychological defense one step beyond resignation is consolation. Consolation can be roughly divided into two types, that sought in human society and that found in nature.

Seeking consolation in nature differs from seeing life reflected in nature. It is, rather, the search for a momentary consolation for the unhappiness of human society by finding refuge in nature. Kenkō straightforwardly expressed this inclination of the Japanese: "In many cases it is helpful to gaze at the moon . . . for whatever suits the particular occasion touches the feelings most. . . . Will not our

---

24. Oda Sakunosuke, *Sesō* [A Phase of Life] (Tokyo: Chūō Kōron Sha, 1948).

hearts therefore be cheered by a lonely ramble in places far from humanity where weeds grow in the pure water?"[25]

Finding consolation for the unhappiness of life by seeking shelter in nature far from humanity is not unique to Japan. But the use of such a view in precepts of life is characteristic of the Japanese view of nature.

One example is found in Ekiken's *Instructions for Ease*: "When one goes on a journey to other provinces and faces a scenic spot or the beauties of nature, it will help one to regain one's conscience and wash away one's stinginess."[26] Ekiken was a man who could find pleasure in anything, and he encouraged fleeing to nature: "If one can perceive the beauties of all creation, one's pleasure is limitless. . . . Since one can be the master of the mountains, waters, moon, and flowers, one need no longer beg or ask for the help of others. Inasmuch as these cannot be bought with money, one does not have to spend even a penny. . . . This pleasure is available even to the poor and humble, and it incurs no future trouble."[27] In brief, he recommended appreciation of the beauties of all creation even to the poor, such as the pleasure of not spending even a penny, of begging, or not asking for the help of others.

Nishikawa Joken also said, in *Lot of the Peasant*, that the beautiful scenes of nature hardly observable in cities were a consolation to peasants. He elucidated this consolation to peasants by quoting the following *waka* poems, calling them "gracious poems composed for peasants and farmhouses":

> Though no place is distasteful,
> Especially the moon
>   shining over the hut laid waste

---

25. William N. Porter, trans., *The Miscellany of a Japanese Priest* (London: Humphrey Milford, 1914), p. 24.
26. Kaibara, *Instructions for Ease*.
27. Ibid.

Is clear and bright.
        Saigyō Hōshi

I only long for
        the moon looked at from a straw-thatched hut,
For she is shaded
        by the lofty palace.
        Go-kashiwabara-in[28]

Many popular songs and *rōkyoku* chants sing of consolation in nature. Kunisada Chūji on his flight from Mount Akagi saw the beauties of nature as the sole consolation for his mishaps: "Ah, it's certainly fine scenery! I still retain a lingering desire for this world, in spite of my wandering self and my intention to shun others' eyes, for I feel pleasure in possessing the moon, snow, and flowers."[29] For the nature-loving Japanese, there is no consolation like fleeing human society and taking nature as their sole possession.

There Is Always Someone Less Fortunate

The escape into nature, however, is a consolation available only to those who still have room for appreciation. On the other hand, in order to obtain consolation in human society, a man has to be imbued with the idea that not only is he unhappy but others are also undergoing bitter or worse experiences. Let me call this sort of consolation, comparing one's life with the lives of others and obtaining comfort from it, consolation by comparison.

Kaibara Ekiken called this comparative method, in which a man

---

28. Nishikawa Joken, *Hyakushō bukuro* [Lot of the Peasant] (1721).

29. Chichibu Shigetake, "Oboro zukiyo chūji tabisugata" ["Chuji's Flight under a Misty Moon"]
    Kunisada Chūji (1810–1850) was a *yakuza* boss who led a life of gambling, fighting, and killing. He was executed in 1850 on a charge of breaking through the checking station at Maebashi in 1836.

comforts himself when he feels unhappy by thinking of more unfortunate people, an important art of the mind or *shinjutsu*: "When
you are unlucky and suffer some misfortune, fall victim to a false
charge, or are treated inhumanely and discourteously by your lord,
parents, brothers, and friends, you must be at ease at heart and not
bothered in mind. Do this by comparing yourself with those who,
in the past in Japan and in China, met a much more bitter misfortune
than yours."[30]

In another book, Ekiken said the comparative method was quite
effective and that everyone, wise and mediocre alike, could make
use of it, for it was an easy resource: "When you suffer misfortune,
think of those who in any age have suffered mishaps. If you would
compare your unhappiness with theirs, you would think that yours
is not so bad and you would have no resentment. . . . When I used
this method, I had good results many times. I can hardly give up
this resource."[31]

In *Precepts for the Warrior*, a book on self-cultivation for warriors,
the comparative method is said to be a *shinjutsu* to cope with a hard
lot: "Recall men in old times who suffered mishaps, or compare
yourself with lesser men who suffer more distresses, and comfort
your mind."[32]

Commoners were told to think of the distresses of the higher ranks,
not of the lower, and to take their own sufferings as nothing. Hakuin,
in *Contentment in the Peaceful Reign*, preached the following song to
the masses under the control of the Tokugawa shogunate: "When
we compare the distresses of the higher ranking people with ours,
ours are nothing, hardly worth counting as man's. Since we are not
even on the level of a horsefly, our sufferings, no matter how severe
they may be, are in no way comparable to theirs."[33]

As the masses were not worth counting as human beings and were

---

30. Kaibara Ekiken, *Yamato zokukun* [Popular Morals of Japan] (1708).
31. Kaibara, *Instructions for Ease*.
32. Izawa Nagahide, *Bushikun* [Precepts for the Warrior] (1715).
33. Hakuin, *Miyo no haratsuzumi* [Contentment in the Peaceful Reign] (c. 1750).

inferior even to flies, no distress was unbearable. It is a well-known fact, according to Tanaka Kyūgu and others, that the farmers of the Tokugawa period were treated as if they were oxen and horses.[34] In the song quoted above they were described as beings inferior to a horsefly. If this were so, they had no lesser beings to compare themselves with, only higher ones.

Nishikawa Joken, however, in his *Lot of the Townsman*, explained the consolation found in looking at a lower level by quoting a *waka* poem: "Though I become wishful as I look up higher, there are many who are not even on my level."[35] The poem is said to have been a recast of the words of Tokugawa Ieyasu, "Don't look up, look down," a maxim repeatedly used by the townsmen of the Tokugawa period.

An Ōmi merchant, Fuwa Yasaburō, wrote a personal note at the end of an inventory book which admonished, "Man should be contented with his lot by looking at a lower level. He should think that if he looked higher, he would, before scheming to make money, only count results and would become a man who only indulges in fancies."[36] This is obviously a state of mind which seeks consolation in the sense of superiority obtained by looking at people on a lower level.

In *Instructions for the Farming Household* the peasants' envy of the townsmen was denounced using the comparative method: "If you are born in a farming village, don't be envious of the bearing of townsmen. The peasants are meager in bearing, yet their minds are not lowly. The townsmen are refined in bearing, yet their minds are lowly, for they judge everything in terms of mere gain. Don't be envious of the prosperity of the rich and noble just because you were born among the poor and humble."[37]

---

34. Tanaka Kyūgu, *Minka bunryōki* [Instruction for the Farming Household] (1721).
35. Nishikawa Joken, *Chōnin bukuro* [Lot of the Townsman] (1719).
36. Fuwa Yasaburō, note (1802).
37. Tanaka, *Instructions for the Farming Household*.

What is said here is that since the farmers are nobler in spirit, they should be content with that. This sort of consolation is mentioned even in current books on self-cultivation. For example, Tomomatsu Entai said, "There is no end in looking downward, nor in looking upward. I always stay between the two. Those who rest between the two are fortunate people. I am indebted to the lower levels."[38]

Consolation through comparison has exerted wide influence socially as an important element of mass entertainment. The *haha-mono* (motion pictures depicting maternal love) and *namida-mono* (motion pictures which move spectators to tears) of the Japanese cinema show the screen characters in situations similar to or less fortunate than those of most of the female spectators.

It is not merely sympathy or fellow feeling but an element of consolation by comparison which attracts a large number of fans. In popular literature, too, the unhappiness of woman is often the theme of novels in women's magazines. To weep, being deeply moved, is the revelation of a sense of shared unhappiness; not only is the reader unfortunate but the heroine of this work is also unfortunate, and the reader is comforted by the conclusion that, on the whole, the life of woman is dogged with unhappiness.

> I should comfort myself
>   by perceiving what the way of the world is,
> For I am not the only one
>   who lives in this floating world.[39]

An attitude like Kenkō's, expressed in this *waka* poem, draws unfortunate women in Japan towards *namida-mono* and *haha-mono* even now.

---

38. Tomomatsu Entai, *Mukuyuru kokoro* [A Grateful Mind] (Tokyo: Jitsugyō no Nihonsha, 1941).
39. Yoshida Kenkō, *Tsurezuregusa* [Essays in Idleness] (1330–1331).

"Knowing How Foolish a Yakuza Is"

The feeling of not even being included in the human race seen in the consolation by comparison advocated by Hakuin does not rest only upon self-abasement in a low social status or in poverty. If a man is imbued with the idea that he is a man is the shadows or a rogue, he is able to bear any experience he undergoes, no matter how bitter, taking it as punishment imposed upon him. This is an attempt to get around a sense of unhappiness by self-reproach or self-incrimination. Needless to say, it is not a matter of actual guilt or innocence but one of self-persuasion that makes the person believe he is guilty.

The *yakuza* (gamblers depicted in popular literature, plays, and movies) are apt to explain their misfortune with such desperate and self-incriminatory words as "What does it matter after all" or "I don't care." This self-incriminatory, tragic resolution appeals to the masses.

A fellow feeling and sympathy for the man in the shadows and the outcast must be latent in the minds of the general public. Historically speaking, the masses of Japan, up to the present, have been neglected and treated as men in the shadows by the authority of the day. Therefore, antisocial men or conduct aroused the sympathy of the masses as symbols of rebellion against that authority. Although such men may not have been aware of it, their unhappiness was looked upon with sympathetic eyes.

Moreover, antisocial men abase themselves as outcasts and take any mishap as punishment due them. This tendency is always an adjunct of the *yakuza* psychology which is favorably depicted in mass entertainment. *Yakuza*, almost without exception, are aware of being fugitives from justice, fools, and oddities and have a deep sense of self-scorn, embodied in the words, "what does it matter after all."

From this self-scorn arises a sense of self-incrimination; instead of grieving over or getting angry at unhappiness and misfortune, one accuses oneself and imposes a punishment for one's foolishness. In his *rōkyoku* chant, "Asataro under the Moon," Hata Kiyoji says, "Knowing how foolish a yakuza is, I know I'm really sinful. Please forgive your uncle, boy. No matter how you look after me, I can't introduce myself to you, for I'm not fit to be seen." *Yakuza*, because they consider themselves social outcasts, believe that they do not deserve to indulge in the happiness that ordinary people find in daily living. The pleasure of being human, the pleasure of love between parent and child, is, to the *yakuza*, too good a happiness. *Yakuza* have to be contented with what they are allotted, for they have intentionally chosen the way of unhappiness. A fugitive from justice is always dogged with a deep sorrow, bearing unhappiness in life.

Kunitarō of Kajikazawa returned to his old home, hoping to meet his mother and his only son, Yasuke, but his mother told him,

> "Whatever your reason may be,
>   I can't tell my dear grandson
>   that his blood father is a fugitive from justice."
> "Ah, forgive me, forgive me,
>   how stupid I am to have come
>   home shamelessly,
>   blinded by a wish to see my child."
>   Hata Kiyoji, "The River Fuefuki Shining
>   under the New Moon"

The fact that he is overcome with affection further deepens his sense of self-incrimination, and he abases himself as a fool.

Shōtarō of Ina recalls a scene at his old home: "Wishing to catch even a glance of my mother, what a fool I am, coming home carelessly! Just like me, a fugitive from justice! It's my fault for being drawn by worldly desires and coming home." (Hata Kiyoji, "Inabushi *Yakuza*")

Yakuza are, in many cases, not allowed to be happy even in romance. "A *yakuza*, after all, shouldn't be in love with a girl. . . .

Otsuyu, take a decent husband as soon as you can. . . . I wish you to be fine and happy. If fate so ordains, let us meet again." (Hata Kiyoji, "Genta of Ejiri")

The *yakuza* feeling of inferiority is a psychological support for bearing unhappiness. The same is true with heroic men who are addressed as boss among *yakuza*. Kunisada Chūji, for example, is delineated as a man who possessed an awareness of his low status. "I'm a jobless *yakuza*. Though I couldn't stand to make myself a mere spectator of the misery of the farming people to whom I am much indebted, I, Chūji, have transgressed the state law. I am a great offender. . . . In the long run, the crime of breaking through a checking station will someday chain me. I, Chūji, am a wanted man. . . . It would bring punishment upon me if I took money in addition to your kind help."[40]

Similarly, those who have committed a crime have a peculiar sense of self-incrimination, feeling that they would be punished if they were to avail themselves of another's kindness. To *yakuza*, in brief, their unhappiness is a matter of course, and their *jingi* (moral code) is to endure their plight and to maintain human relationships fettered by *giri* (obligation) and *on* (a debt of gratitude).

A tragedy caused by self-incrimination is, then, felt by the masses to be a familiar situation in their own unhappy daily lives. Dazai Osamu in *No Longer Human* often touches upon the current awareness of the man in the shadows, a position similar to that of the *yakuza*. He writes of the tragedy of a man who attributes the cause of unhappiness to his vice: "All my unhappiness is a result of my vice. . . . Am I, as is said in common talk, an egoist? Or am I, on the contrary, too timid? I myself don't know for sure. Anyway, as I seem to be vice personified, I make myself endlessly unhappy and I have no way to stop."[41]

---

40. Chichibu Shigetake, "Ninjō tsuki no yobanashi" ["Story Told on a Moonlit Night"].

41. Dazai Osamu, *Ningen shikkaku* [No Longer Human] (Tokyo: Chikuma Shobō, 1948).

Originally, Dazai's sense of self-incrimination resulted from asking whether the life of an antisocial man in the shadows might not be more honest, for he was "afraid of the so-called legitimacy in the world," which is filled with "cases of clean, bright, cheerful distrust."[42] To Dazai, therefore, his onetime participation in the leftist movement was a result of a fellow feeling for "illegitimacy . . . the man in the shadows . . . criminal consciousness . . . the fugitive from justice" and his response to the disposition of the movement rather than its primary aim.[43] He sensed that as long as he submerged himself in the world of illegitimacy, in which everyone was subject to unhappiness and misfortune, he would not have to suffer among the people in legitimate society.

This is similar to Nagai Kafū's view of a man in the shadows as one cut off from society. "I am one who has long since been forsaken by the austere people of the world. Since the children of my relatives no longer come to see me, I scarcely have to defer to them."[44]

To Kafū, as a bachelor in *The Flower in the Shade* says, "the life of the people who have honor and dignity, though I have no reason to think so, seems to be constrained and hypocritical."[45] He came to find humanity in "women who live in the shadows and who feel neither fear nor hatred but rather friendliness and affection when they encounter men who must avoid the public eye."[46]

Dazai said that he could have a "heart so tender as to be enraptured" by people in the shadows.[47] His words are the most precise exhibition of the sense of unhappiness and self-incrimination characteristic of the Japanese in finding humanity and beauty only in

---

42. Ibid.
43. Ibid.
44. Nagai Kafū, *Bokutō kidan* [A Strange Tale from East of the River] (Tokyo: Asahi Shimbun Sha, 1937).
45. Nagai Kafū, *Hikage no hana* [The Flower in the Shade] (Tokyo: Chūō Kōron Sha, 1934).
46. Nagai, *Strange Tale*.
47. Dazai, *No Longer Human*.

unhappiness. Like Dazai, the masses are enraptured by the state of mind of the *yakuza*, as they listen to *rōkyoku* chants and popular songs.

In this reaction to unhappiness, only its negative aspects are acknowledged; no attempt is made to recognize a positive value in it. On the other hand, the positive psychological solution is an attempt to find some value in unhappiness, to rationalize it away. It is paradoxical to think that unhappiness is, in actuality, something desirable.

This positive solution includes the idea that unhappiness offers a good opportunity for self-cultivation and service. In relation to the belief that happiness is hazardous and transient, it acknowledges unhappiness as safer and adversity as preferable. When this view is taken one step further, it develops into a morality and an aesthetics of imperfectionism unique to Japan: everything is preferable and beautiful in a state of imperfection or incompletion.

Pain Will Naturally Turn Out to Be Pleasure

The view that poverty is highly appropriate for self-cultivation has traditionally been expounded. Ekiken's *Instructions for Ease* is representative of this view: "Since the poor and humble are less negligent, they are easy to remonstrate with. The rich and noble, due to their infatuation with transient affairs of the world, do not know how to enjoy reading and the Way. Thus, to be rich and noble is to be unhappy."[48]

Moving on from the theory of honest poverty, Ekiken arrived at the paradox that unhappy things are happy: "It is easy to be in favorable circumstances, but it is hard to be in unfavorable circumstances. Therefore, if you are in unfavorable circumstances, since you will learn respect and veneration, you will make fewer mistakes

---

48. Kaibara, *Instructions for Ease.*

and will become happier."[49] This is a more positive reaction to unhappiness than the theory of honest poverty. If being in unfavorable
circumstances is good for self-cultivation, how should one view
efforts to overcome adversity? This theory also consoles those who
can never pull themselves out of adversity.

The argument that even one's ugly countenance should be a
cause for happiness because it averts depravity arises from this point
of view. Miura Baien said, "Although man's appearance is bestowed
by Heaven, good-looking men and women are apt to be enticed
by many. The more enticers they have, the greater their chances to
be unchaste. Plain men and women have fewer enticers. The fewer
enticers they have, the fewer are their chances to be unchaste."[50]

Nishikawa Joken's statement that farmers leading lives filled
with pain are serving society, and are therefore treasures of the
state, parallels the attitude that one is fortunate to have adversity.
Joken, after disclosing the vices of wealthy townsmen, stated, "It
is said that 'Poverty is the god of wealth.' Cultivating fields, building houses, fishing, boating, drawing water, gathering firewood,
and so forth are all the work of the poor; therefore, the poor are
the precious treasures of the state. There is no greater god of wealth
than the poor."[51]

Not only in this statement but in other writings, Joken often said
that the pain imposed upon the farmers would turn out to be
pleasure if they could endure it. For example, he said: "Certainly,
peasants must always have chances to amuse themselves by watching
the growing rice, wheat, and fruit, which exceed the beauty of flowers and crimson leaves. All pleasures in the human world are latent
in pain. If you are weary of pain, your pain gets increasingly severe.
You ought to see pain as constantly attendant on man, a provisional
lodger in the human world. You should try neither to cast away pain

---

49. Ibid.
50. Miura Baien, *Baien sōsho* [A Baien Series] (1750).
51. Nishikawa, *Lot of the Peasant*.

nor to chase after pleasure, and pain will naturally turn out to be pleasure."[52]

Joken thus arrived at the paradox that pain is pleasure by progressing from the idea that adversity is fortune. It is not simply seeing joy in labor but is a more philosophical theory on the concurrence of pain and pleasure, stemming from an outlook which sees pain as constantly attendant on man. Joken, in a passage where he explains the happiness of farmers in their situation, said: "Seeing that pain always follows man, a person ought not to take it as pain. The first cry of a newborn baby is the beginning of pain. He suffers, so he cries. Days later, he laughs for the first time. Isn't this the logic of nature, that man is always shadowed first by pain, then by pleasure? Pain is pain for the Emperor, not to mention the four classes of people below him. If you bear this in mind, there is no difference between pain and pleasure."[53] Thus, he came to the conclusion that all pleasure in the human world is latent in pain.

Even at the present time, the logic that adversity is good for self-cultivation is used in various books on the subject. A typical book states, "He who suffers is happy because he comes to realize the profundity of life and the good things in life. The more scanty goods become, the more regard is paid to food and clothing."[54] The logic that suffering is happiness is a variation of the view that pain is food for pleasure and does not end in pain but is to some extent rewarded.

The theory that adversity is happiness, although it emphasizes self-cultivation, has some positive elements. It not only expounds endless endurance but also gives hope; it brings some elements to bear upon the principle of success in life or happiness. In the case of Japan, however, the principle of success in life differs, for instance, from that of America in one respect. In Japan the idea of success in life is that one should not be inspired by upward-looking emulation but that one will be rewarded by undergoing hardships in one's present situation

---

52. Ibid.
53. Ibid.
54. Tomomatsu, *A Grateful Mind.*

without looking upward. An example can be found in the *Tōkyū-jutsu* (a system of astrology), which cites a saying accredited to Tokugawa Ieyasu concerning his success: "The important thing is to put on a big *daikoku-zukin* (a cap shaped something like a tam-o'-shanter) and not look upward but toil. . . . Indeed, if one puts on a big *daikoku-zukin*, he cannot see upward. If he cannot see upward, he will feel no envy. If he feels no envy, he will attend closely to his trade, for he has nothing to distract his attention."

Know How to Be Content

The psychological solution to unhappiness, when taken one step further, becomes a principle of contentment and comfort: if one puts up with unhappiness and insufficiency, the resulting state of contentment becomes comfort. This is not seeing contentment as a kind of self-cultivation but enjoying the state of contentment itself positively. The psychology in this stage is no longer normal but is similar to masochism, in which gratification deepens with torment. It might be called Japanese masochism.

Chōmei, in *An Account of My Hut*, said, "Knowing myself and the world, I have no ambitions and do not mix in the world. I seek only tranquility; I rejoice in the absence of grief."[55] This is a revelation of the view of contentment and comfort.

In *Essays in Idleness* the joy of contentment is also described: "It is best for a man to be thrifty, to shrink from luxuries, not to accumulate great wealth, and not to covet the whole world. The great men of ancient times were seldom rich."[56]

Further, if a man lives a retiring life, he will involuntarily arrive at contentment: "For indeed when one has once wearied of this life and has set out upon the Way, even if he has still some desires, there

---

55. Donald Keene, ed., *Anthology of Japanese Literature, from the Earliest Era to the Mid-Nineteenth Century* (New York: Grove Press, 1955), p. 210.
56. Porter, *Miscellany*, p. 20.

is no comparison between his condition and the great cupidity of a man of the world. . . . His wants are but scanty, his heart will quickly be satisfied."[57]

This, in fine, signifies that the less one wants and clings to, the more easily one is satisfied. The state of contentment and comfort is, therefore, not ascetic; rather, it is a mental device with which one limits one's objectives in advance and facilitates the satisfaction of one's wants. In short, it is not to suppress one's present wants but to place oneself in a situation where there are fewer factors leading to wants and temptation. Therefore, Kenkō had no confidence that he could become one of "the great recluses while hiding amidst a town" and letting himself dwell amid every possible temptation. Taking oneself away from temptation is a precautionary measure resulting from a weakness in the will to control wants. Kenkō's actual materialism is clearly visible.

Chōmei exhibits a similar state of mind. In fact, Chōmei did not retire for ascetic penance or for self-cultivation; on the contrary, he attempted to live at his ease by fleeing from the world of anxiety and a precarious life. In that respect he could be said to have been a sort of negative hedonist. His statement at the end of *An Account of My Hut* is an example of this: "The essence of the Buddha's teaching to man is that we must not have attachment for any object. It is a sin for me now to love my little hut, and my attachment to its solitude may also be a hindrance to salvation. Why should I waste more precious time in relating such trifling pleasures?"[58]

In other words, both Kenkō and Chōmei could live at their ease, avoiding social or family life. The masses, however, have long been forced to live in the midst of towns filled with temptation, indoctrinated with the idea, "Know how to be contented," and have been forced to put it into practice.

---

57. Ibid., p. 51.
58. Keene, *Anthology*, p. 211.

Even when Ekiken preached the idea, "Once you know how to be contented, you will enjoy life even if you are poor and humble,"[59] people only knew that there was pleasure even in needy circumstances and that there were times when they could not indulge in enjoyment even if they were blessed materially. Pleasure in this case means "no anxiety" and does not refer to positive gratification. The very meaning of the Japanese word *anraku*, "pleasure," connotes only a rudimentary *anshin*, "comfort."

This attitude toward contentment and comfort was also adopted by warriors. This is obvious in the poems in *A Record of Vital Contrivances* written by Udono Chōkai in the latter part of the Tokugawa period.

> If people live
>   not looking upward but knowing their lot,
> Warriors, farmers, artisans, and merchants,
>   all will live at ease.
> He who knows
>   how to be contented in everything
>   and to be patient with life
> Will live in comfort.[60]

"The vital thing is to know your lot and to forbear in all matters."

An analogous idea is revealed in an essay on the lot of the townsman. Nishikawa Joken wrote, "The townsmen should stay down, not outclassing the upper classes. They ought not to be envious of the powerful. If they live in simplicity and frugality, are contented with their lot, and enjoy the birds-of-a-feather-flock-together life, then their pleasures in life will never run out."[61]

What Joken meant by the comfort of the townsmen, however, can not be detected by looking superficially at these lines. As we

---

59. Kaibara, *Instructions for Ease.*
60. Udono Chōkai, *Kanyō kufūroku* [A Record of Vital Contrivances] (1812).
61. Nishikawa Joken, *Chōnin bukuro* [Lot of the Townsman] (1719).

will see later, the life of the warrior did not seem comfortable to Joken. The birds-of-a-feather-flock-together pleasures of the towns-men were, in fact, not simply negative contentment and comfort. Joken also talked of the pleasures of the peasants, which contrasted with the townsmen's pleasures: "Since townsmen in many cases suddenly become wealthy, there are many chances for them to lose their wealth. Since peasants are less blessed with chances to become rich, they do not lose their wealth so suddenly. Regardless of what you are, if you are contented with your lot and rest peacefully upon your status, your pleasures will never be exhausted."[62]

Farmers were thus subject only to negative comforts, not liable to sudden loss. Joken, using the tenet of the accordance of pain and pleasure, professed that if even the Emperor has pain, how much more true this must be of the lower classes: "If you are thankful for being born in a farmhouse, if you have nothing to distract your mind, and enjoy what you are, no pleasure can compare with this. As pain always shadows man, you must not take it as pain. . . . Pain is pain for the Emperor, not to mention the four classes. If you bear this in mind, there is no difference between pain and pleasure."[63]

Joken's philosophy of contentment and comfort differs in both means and content from the discourses of other moralists, such as Ekiken, for he attempts to find comfort in the differences between social classes.

The result of contentment is individual comfort, after all a kind of hedonism. This differs from the negative solution to unhappiness, for it has a positive quality. On that score, Ekiken says in *Instructions for the Preservation of Health*, "Pleasure is an innate constitution of the individual, the physiology of the universe. . . . Losing no pleasure is the basis of preservation of health."[64]

Ekiken regarded the mind as the master of body and emphasized comfort of mind, saying, "Let the mind be at ease. The body is the

---

62. Ibid.
63. Ibid.
64. Kaibara Ekiken, *Yōjōkun* [Instructions for the Preservation of Health] (1713).

servant of the mind. Let the body toil."[65] At the same time, he cited the "three pleasures . . . to be enjoyed by man . . . enjoyment of goodness, . . . good health, . . . long life."[66] "Comfort" does not signify only spiritual pleasure. Since he sees pleasure as the chief object of self-cultivation, his view is a type of hedonism. It is interesting that many Japanese books on self-cultivation, not only Ekiken's, contain philosophies based on *nikutai-shugi* (physicality), that is, good conduct or going into service are regarded as good for the health.

In *Notes by Shibuya Okinokami*, for instance, it is said that if a warrior were contented with his lot in service, he would live a long time. "He who serves in return for his lord's favor has neither discontent nor grudge, even if he is never promoted. Such a man lives long and his mind is at ease, for he accords naturally to the rule of Heaven."[67]

In brief, the healthful effects of this state of self-complacency accompanied by a sense of gratitude have been accentuated. This emphasis shows the practicality of the way of the warrior rather than its morality. The treatise on contentment and comfort has been forced on the Japanese people by every possible means, from didactic songs of the Tokugawa period which said "The initiation of comfort is but to know how to be contented" and "Rice and soup and cotton cloth are necessities, but other goods only molest me," to the imperative preachment of the more modern *Tōkyū-jutsu*, "Heaven does not give two gifts simulaneously. Man should not complain, for all things are apt to lack something."[68]

Even now this view of contentment and comfort is adopted by people on different social levels with various interpretations. Ozu Kinosuke of the Ozu *yakuza* group "did not feel any inconvenience for a long time" in a solitary cell. He claims to have found that "if

---

65. Ibid.
66. Ibid.
67. Shibuya Okinokami, *Shibuya Okinokami hikki* [Notes by Shibuya Okinokami] (1749).
68. Yōshin-dō and Shōyō-do, *Toky-ūjutsu kōwa* [A System of Astrology] (Tokyo: Eirakudōn, 1912).

I applied a simplified view of life based on contentment and comfort in the actual world, I could undoubtedly live in peace. I would neither have to struggle for a living nor fear earthquakes and fires. All I would have to do is to escape only with my very body."[69]

The Japanese people have acquired the conviction that it is sufficient and less constraining for them if they keep only the necessities of life at hand. The masses are always haunted, whether in war or peace, by uneasiness at the thought of being driven into a state of emergency. A preference for having nothing to be encumbered with is not only ascribable to the idea of contentment with one's assigned lot or to frugality rather than indulgence in luxury; it follows from the lame logic of self-complacency, that one is carefree if one has nothing to lose. A passage in a Buddhist text on self-cultivation makes good use of this psychology: "It is therefore necessary to train yourself to comply with frugal and simplified living, bearing hardship and privation and avoiding as much as possible being drawn into a struggle for living."[70] The knowledge of contentment is recommended on the same basis as providing psychological immunity from unhappiness.

Similarly, a poem in the *Tōkyū-jutsu* which sounds like a parody of a Buddhist *sutra* exhorts the reader to know contentment. It is a humorous yet somehow pitiful didactic poem:

> Go make yourself a guest if you want a house.
> Go on an excursion if you want a garden.
> Mountains, seas, rivers, and hills, all are yours as
>   long as you feast your eyes on them. If you are spiritless
>   in this broad world, you cannot live a life worth living.
> Isn't it enough to have a one-mat space to sleep in?
> Life is enjoyable if you know your lot.[71]

69. Ozu Kinosuke, *Shin yakuza monogatari* [A New *Yakuza* Story] (Tokyo: Hayakawa Shobō, 1953).
70. Tomomatsu, *A Grateful Mind.*
71. Yōshin-dō and Shōyō-dō, *A System of Astrology.*

The Best Love Is Secret Love

The next step is a psychology rooted in insufficiency, which finds value in a lack of perfection. This attitude deems insufficiency and discontent more valuable than sufficiency and content and is characteristic of the Japanese.

There must be many arguments as to when and how this concept originated in Japan. It is, however, obvious that it has a bearing on the Japanese views of impermanency and contentment which I have discussed.

Kenkō was the first to distinctly express this philosophy. It consists of finding and enjoying an insufficient and imperfect thing rather than a perfect thing. The idea is put forth in that famous section beginning with the passage: "Is it only when the flowers are in full bloom and when the moon is shining in spotless perfection that we ought to gaze at them?"[72]

Ultimately, the idea is derived from the futility of expecting something to be perfect. In the words of Kenkō, "the perfect circle of the full moon lasts only for a very short time; soon it begins to wane."[73] Such proverbs as "Waxing and waning are the custom of the world" and "Meeting is the beginning of parting" show that perfect things do not last long and are transient. One will sooner find satisfaction in insufficiency than in perfection and can thus avoid being driven to despair.

In short, if one becomes immune to insufficiency, the lack of perfection, he will neither be disappointed nor become desperate in case of emergency. This is an extended form of the aforementioned immunity to unhappiness.

This idea is also applicable to romantic love. "The love of sweet-

---

72. Porter, *Miscellany*, p. 105.
73. Ibid., p. 182.

hearts when they can see each other without interruption is hardly worthy of mention. But when they are sadly prevented from meeting, when they are troubled by their engagement being all in vain, when, spending the long night alone, their thoughts fly to the faraway clouds and the regretted days of old in their now deserted hut, then indeed may they be said to know what love is."[74]

Kenkō objects to marriage, the perfection of love, on these grounds. "What is generally known as a wife is a thing no man should have. I like to hear a man say, 'I live ever as a bachelor.' . . . Whatever kind of a woman she be, if he keeps seeing her about him from morn till eve, his heart grows weary and he begins to dislike her; the woman herself too becomes inattentive. To live apart therefore and to go and stay with her from time to time is the way to form a tie that the passing months and years can never dissolve; for it will be no affliction then for him to go and pay her a little visit."[75]

Cultivation of an attitude of not believing in or expecting anything is hidden behind Kenkō's imperfectionism. Therefore he says, "Many are the things on which we should place no reliance; for it is because he had had such complete confidence in them that a foolish man feels angry and resentful when they fail him. . . . If you base your hopes neither on yourself nor on others, then if good comes your way you will rejoice, and if evil you will not repine."[76] The state in which a person places no reliance on things can be attained by contemplating the impermanency of life. "None knows the time of death; it comes not from in front, but ever presses on from behind. All men know indeed the fact of death, but as they do not realize its urgency it finally comes upon them unexpectedly. When the sands are dry the sea appears very far away; but ere long the flowing tide will sweep up over the shore. . . . You may pamper your body as you will, but what can you expect at the appointed time save old age and death? Swiftly they approach and do not delay

74. Ibid., p. 106.
75. Ibid., pp. 147–48.
76. Ibid., p. 158.

their coming even for a moment."[77] Every man is thus deprived of his life by death ever pressing on from behind, coming without any advance notice.

The sole means of overcoming unpredictable fear and unease, not the fear coming from in front in the daytime but the fear from behind out of the darkness, is to constantly contemplate death rather than life, to anticipate unhappiness rather than happiness, and to expect imperfection and insufficiency rather than perfection and sufficiency. This is the psychological basis of "insufficiency-ism."

If the transiency and imperfection derived from uncertainty about the length of life are far better than permanence and perfection, an attitude which finds beauty in insufficiency arises: "The dew upon Adashi Moor never fades away, nor is Toribe Moor ever free from smoke; what a state of things we should have, were our existence never to be cut short! There would be no feelings of pity left in the world. Far better is it to have no certainty as to the length of life."[78] This is the high point of Kenkō's imperfectionism. He often speaks of the essential beauty found in insufficiency and imperfection: "But Tona says, 'Thin silk (book covers) frayed at the top and the bottom, and mother-of-pearl inlaid picture rollers from which the shell has dropped out are the best,' is not that a charming sentiment? . . . But Archdeacon Kōyū says, 'Things which are made all exactly the same are doubtless the work of those who have but little taste; 'tis better to have dissimilarity'; and he is certainly right. Generally speaking, uniformity in anything at all is bad."[79]

Aesthetic thought based on imperfectionism was propounded not only by Kenkō. Many studies have been made on *yūgen* (mystic profundity), *wabi* (serene taste), and *sabi* (calm and simple taste; literally, mellowed by use), which belong to the same aesthetic family, as important conventions in the history of Japanese art. I have

---

77. Ibid., pp. 122, 63.
78. Ibid., p. 13.
79. Ibid., p. 67.

quoted Kenkō because his argument seems to express the psychological basis of imperfectionism most clearly.

Shōtetsu, a medieval poet, writing in the aforementioned *Shōtetsu's Talks*, deems Kenkō's imperfectionism an innate psychology common to all. "There is hardly a man who has an inner desire to see things only in perfection, for, as Kenkō asked, 'Is it only when the flowers are in full bloom and when the moon is shining in spotless perfection that we ought to gaze at them?' This desire [to see things in imperfection] is innate."[80]

He also talks of *yūgen* as "something drifting, inexpressible in words," a state of mind "not clearly expressed by words implying certain intentions." He says that "a poem leaving something unmentioned is a good poem."[81] That is, the inexpressible and unmentioned are not in the words of a poem but in the mind of a poet. Thus Shōtetsu finds beauty in insufficiency which leaves something unmentioned in a poem. The "so-called *yūgen* rests in the mind but is inexpressible in words" and "it is a state hardly definable as tasteful or exquisite."[82] *Yūgen* perceives beauty not in things distinctly and fully appealing to our senses, but in things lost in obscurity. The beauty of imperfect things has elements in common with the indirect expression and uncertain beauty characteristic of Japanese art.

Imperfectionism is thus related to the concept of beauty called *yūgen*. On the other hand, it has brought forth a psychological tradition in which, as Kenkō said, hopeless love or forbearing and secret love is highly valued, as opposed to full expression of one's affection. This suppression of feelings, together with the Japanese sense of unhappiness, is a source of Japanese masochism.

Sōgi, a linked-verse poet, took pleasure in composing poems on suppressed love feelings. In his comment on the *Collection of Poems Ancient and Modern* he praised poems tinged with this sentiment

---

80. Shōtetsu, *Shōtetsu monogatari* [Shōtetsu's Talks] (1430).
81. Ibid.
82. Ibid.

which used such expressions as "ardent mind," "pitiful mind," and "deeply emotional."[83]

The longer a feeling is suppressed, the purer and firmer it becomes: this is the Japanese theory. This is entirely different from the western view. Especially since the Renaissance, purification and intensification of feeling have been cultivated through free expression. Westerners feel that the longer a feeling is repressed, the poorer and drier it becomes. According to the Japanese theory, however, the longer a feeling is suppressed, the more its potential energy increases. This is one of the traditional psychological elements of Japanese art which, as seen in *noh*, is a basis for the efforts made to heighten one's innermost feelings while suppressing their outward manifestations as much as possible.

As the *haiku* poet, Kyoroku, says in his *haibun* (prose accompanying *haiku* poems) in *Admonishments for Eating, Drinking, and Lust*, "Bafflement is the essence of love. When lovers are unable to meet, they lament over it; when they meet at night, they upbraid a cock for announcing the dawn. In the sound of a bell heard in the evening, waiting for love, the sentiment of love is fully disclosed."[84] The beauty of suppressed love was highly esteemed in the literary thought of the Tokugawa period.

The Japanese aesthetic exemplified in the purity of forbearing love is also discussed in application to the disposition of a warrior's service. The *Hagakure* often stressed that service, as forbearing love, should be carried out wholeheartedly, leaving one's lord unaware of it. "I take it that the highest state of love is forbearing love. If two meet, it would be a lower state of love. The true meaning of love is to die in pining for love all through one's life. A poem reads: 'I will die for love. Let my heart be known after my death, for I will never make manifest the truth of my heart so long as I live.' This is

---

83. Sōgi, *Kokin jikkōshō* [Discourses on the *Kokinshū*] (1501).
84. Kyoroku, "Inshoku shikiyoku no shin ["Admonishments for Eating, Drink]ing, and Lust"] in *Fūzoku monzen* [Anthology of Prose by Haiku Poets] (1706).

what I call sublime love." Such an attitude is "applicable to all dis-
cretions" and "relations between lord and vassal are smoothed by
this attitude of mind." That is, in such a matter as falling in love,
"the more you feel miserable and painful, the more your love
grows. When you happen to meet your love, you feel that you
would not mind even giving up your life for your love. . . . Especially if you do not unbosom yourself throughout your life, you
will become more deeply involved in love. When you meet her
later accidentally, for a while you will rejoice at the chance; however, when you realize it is a chimera, you will pine more for your
love. Relationships between lord and vassal should be in this manner.
The true meaning of service is defined as such."[85]

The attitude evident in forbearing love should be adopted in the
disposition of service; a vassal's loyalty to his lord on account of
a great debt of gratitude or out of respect for his great personality
would not be true service. A proverb says, "Accept your parents and
lord as ones who are unreasonable." To be patient with a lord's un-
reasonableness and exorbitance is true service, just as the true meaning of forlorn love is to endure the cold treatment of one's willful
sweetheart. The *Hagakure* expresses this idea in the following manner: "Nakano Jinemon instructed: 'Your service when your lord
treats you kindly is not true service. Your service when he is merci-
less and ill-treats you is true service. Be fully aware of this point.'
Thus, I have heard, he used to say."[86]

The psychology of imperfectionism is a kind of Japanese masochism; it finds gratification in maltreatment. Isn't the practice of the
bushidō (way of the warrior), at any rate, a cultivation of masochism,
since in it gratification and pleasant sensations are acquired through
the endurance of maltreatment?

As is said in the *Hagakure*, "a true service to a lord is an unrecog-

---

85. Yamamoto, *Shade of Leaves.*
86. Ibid.

nized service, to repay the lord's favors, do good by stealth, and do not expect any return."[87]

Until after the war, military education aimed at inculcating youth with the spirit of unrecognized service of the *Hagakure*. This took the shape of glorification of an unrecognized and unknown death in action. For military men "a sudden death in an unknown spot in the skies of the South Seas or the wilderness of Manchuria or China was said to be honorable. And they were taught not to hope for a glorious death."[88] Therefore, "to be incorporated into the suicide units was a good thing, for unit members were given a chance, though this may sound a bit misleading, for a highly honorable way to die."[89]

This is a confrontation of an honorable death with a death for the sake of service, and in the history of *bushidō* the conflict between these two ways of death must have been pondered continuously.

The Tea Master, a Man of Eccentric Taste

It is in the tea cult that the beauty of insufficiency is most obviously propounded. This is especially true where the tea cult and Zen belief overlap. Jakuan Sōtaku calls this *wabicha*, the quiet taste of drinking tea. This means that the essence of the tea cult is to know how to be contented, how to put up with insufficiency.[90] In *Discourses on Zen and Tea* written by Sōtaku, *wabi* is defined as "a state of material insufficiency, of frustration, and of hard lots," in which "you should never take inconvenience as inconvenience, privation as privation, and lack as lack." To take privation not as

---

87. Ibid.
88. Iizuka, *Japanese Military.*
89. Ibid.
90. Jakuan Sōtaku, *Zencharoku* [Discourses on Zen and Tea] (1828).

privation but "to make frustrating circumstances a pleasure" is the imperfectionism of *Discourses on Zen and Tea*.[91]

In the Tokugawa period, Yanagisawa Kien wrote in his essay, *Miscellany of Floating Thoughts*, that imperfectionism makes shift with something else for lack of good tea utensils and "that all tasteful things can only be experienced in the state of privation."[92]

The imperfectionism of the tea cult is also derived from the view on knowing contentment that is revealed in *An Essay on the Tea Cult as an Aid to Government* written by Ii Naosuke. "If pleasure is not gratification accompanied by a sense of contentment, it is not real pleasure. . . . If each individual is satisfied with his lot and is not envious, he will enjoy life because he knows contentment and will be contented because of enjoying his lot."[93] This is what he calls *suki* (artistic taste) or *wabi*. In other words, "If the art of drinking tea were widely practiced throughout the country . . . both high and low would be content with their lots, would enjoy but not grieve, and would do no wrong. . . . The country would become peaceful and tranquil spontaneously."[94] Here the pragmatic aim is obvious: the imperfectionism of the tea cult becomes an aid to government.

In the present-day tea cult, which values *wabi* and *sabi*, the idea of knowing contentment and resting upon complacency is put forth; this does not differ in the slightest from the discourse of Naosuke. For instance, in *Tea Cult Classroom* written by Sasaki Sanmi after the war, the transition from knowing contentment to imperfectionism is elucidated: "The tea cult stresses 'accordance with one's lot' and 'knowing contentment and resting upon complacency'; it eliminates extravagance and warns against excessiveness. . . . When this state of mind shifts to a positive state of loving privation and taking delight in poverty, *wabicha* arises."

---

91. Ibid.
92. Yanagisawa Kien, *Unpyō sasshi* [Miscellany of Floating Thoughts] (1796).
93. Ii Naosuke, *Sadō no seidō no tasuke to narubeki o agetsuraeru bun* [An Essay on the Tea Cult as an Aid to Government] (1846).
94. Ibid.

Thus, "in the state of finding beauty in imperfect things, modesty begins to function and a love of privation and simplicity develops. . . . Man will come to realize that the highest state is to forsake his self completely. . . . He will attempt to dissolve all his irrelevant ideas called ego and to unite himself with the eternal and infinite universe."[95]

This belief of the tea cult, that the participant moves from the principle of knowing contentment to love of imperfection and further to the dissolution of ego, is a typical example of Japanese self-denial.

Imperfectionism less extreme than this is adopted not only in the tea cult but also in various arts of living. In the *Encyclopedia for the Art of Living*, for example, imperfectionism is said to be necessary not only for art but also for life: "The world of art and *haikai* (seventeen-syllable verse) develops in a state where things are not completely depicted but something is left unmentioned. This is true of life. . . . Life without wastefulness . . . has no lingering impressions. A lack of smoothness is felt. You should do something wasteful and know what *fūryū* (elegance) is. It is said that waxing and waning are the way of the world. This too is channeled to lingering impressions."[96]

These lingering impressions are a mental state; therefore, "to do something wasteful and know what *fūryū* is" must mean living a suitably tasteful life without having to spend money. For the masses, *fūryū* is limited, for example, to hanging a wind-bell from the eaves of the house or to going on a flower-viewing excursion. To put up with such a degree of *fūryū* is the art of living based upon an appreciation of insufficiency. And the Japanese are said to be a people with a sense of *fūryū* and versatile tastes, although they are poor.

Although the effectuation of the propaganda of imperfectionism, which teaches people to find pleasure even in poverty, was so

---

95. Sasaki Sanmi, *Sadō kyōshitsu* [Tea Cult Classroom] (Tokyo: Kōbunsha, 1950).
96. Ōyama, *Encyclopedia*.

successful that the masses learned to get satisfaction from suitable tastes, the philosophy itself was not an outgrowth of the Japanese national character. There emerged one strong objection to the *wabi* and *sabi* of the tea cult in the Tokugawa period. Dazai Shundai, a Confucianist with a rationalistic bent, condemned *wabi* in the tea cult in his essay, *Solitary Words.* "Whatever tea dilettantes do is a copy of the poor and humble. The rich and noble, however, must have a reason to find pleasure in copying the poor and humble. Why should those who are, from the outset, poor and humble further copy the poor and humble and make fun of them?"[97] Shundai must have found the tea cult very distasteful for in another place he criticized it severely: "All that a tea dilettante does is to copy everything which looks poor and shabby."[98]

Shundai's criticism of the curiosity of rich and noble tea dilettantes strikes at the class nature of imperfectionism. There were few criticisms of the tea cult made from this point of view during the Tokugawa period. There did exist more general criticism of the views of knowing contentment through imperfectionism, a more advanced way of thinking close to hedonism.

Pretend to Have No Desire for Money

The imperfectionism seen in Kenkō's and Chōmei's Buddhist views of life and the *samurai* attitude toward service during the Tokugawa period has come to be related to the spirit of austerity of the Shōwa period. Even in the postwar present, it has taken root in the Japanese views on morality and art.

Shundai wrote during the middle of the Tokugawa period, the initial stage of the emergence of antifeudalistic and rationalistic ways of thinking based on commercial capitalism. Views close to rational-

---

97. Dazai Shundai, *Dokugo* [Solitary Words] (1816).
98. Ibid.

ism seen in the schools of Ogyū Sorai and Dazai Shundai in Confucianism and of Mabuchi and Norinaga in Japanese classicism are good examples. These are criticisms of the imperfectionism connected with the feudalistic concept of knowing how to be contented with one's portion in life.

But Motoori Norinaga flatly contradicted Kenkō's philosophy. As one of the representatives of the antifeudal thought which grew up among townsmen during the middle of the Tokugawa period, he took a stand affirming pleasure seeking. In the *Jeweled Bamboo Basket of Essays* he provided a special article entitled "Criticism on Remarks Made by the Monk Kenkō" in which he said, "Who else in his poem would have expressed a wish for wind on the flowers and a cloud over the moon? What that monk said does not accord with human feelings but is a fabricated aesthetic taste formed in the impertinent mind of a man of a later age, and it is not a truly aesthetic taste. What that monk said can be described . . . as contrived only to make what does not accord with human wishes a refined taste."[99]

Norinaga not only rejected any word or way of thinking not in accordance with human desires as a "fabricated thing," but also said, in opposing the hypocrisy of the didacticism of knowing how to be contented, "There is no end to one's making a wish, high or low or moderately. It is a true feeling of the people that there has never been a time when they are really satisfied, yet many talk knowingly as if they knew how to be contented and take pride in it. It must be a fabrication customary with the Chinese."[100]

Norinaga criticized the theory that a poor man is happier than a wealthy man in an article in the *Jeweled Bamboo Basket of Essays* entitled "Criticism on Making a Virtue out of not Wishing for Wealth and Fame." He severely condemned this idea as hypocrisy: "Confucianists of the world regard not worrying about being poor

---

99. Motoori Norinaga, *Tamakatsuma* [Jeweled Bamboo Basket of Essays] (1794–1812).
100. Ibid.

and humble and not wishing for or delighting in prosperity as a virtue, but it is not one's true feeling. It must be the customary line of fabrication formulated by those who covet fame. There may be some who possess such a frame of mind, but they are just eccentric. What's good about it?"[101]

Norinaga said in the same article, connecting positive success with filial piety, "Isn't it true filial piety towards one's parents and ancestors to do all work temperately to the best of one's ability, to raise oneself in the world, and to become wealthy and better off? There is no impiety worse than ruining oneself and impoverishing one's house."[102]

Nishikawa Joken, like Norinaga, might well be counted a representative of the hedonism included in the townsmen's thoughts, in terms of his affirmation of physical pleasure. "A man said, 'There are two types of pleasure. . . . To know the reason of heaven and earth, man and matter, and to enjoy the Way is real pleasure. Eating and drinking, lust and diversion, this is worldly pleasure. . . . How about you, townsman, which do you want to have, real pleasure or worldly pleasure?' I in answer said, 'No matter how I compare them, the so-called real pleasures seem uninteresting. It is the worldly pleasure I prefer.' Thereupon, he burst out laughing, saying, 'How true it is, to realize that the reality of eating and drinking and lust is no less than the real pleasure! Isn't your attitude really interesting?' "[103]

Joken, however, did not support hedonism which seeks after worldly pleasure in eating and drinking, lust and diversion. Prior to the passage quoted above, he cited a man who, in contrast to pleasure, divided pain into two types: "right pain," in which "each component of the four classes should perform his part and keep himself mindful of the five relations," and "the pain of desire," in which "one does not know how to be satisfied and keeps on looking for satisfaction." The man advised that "since real pleasure and right

---

101. Ibid.
102. Ibid.
103. Nishikawa, *Lot of the Townsman*.

pain are heavenly affairs and are in concord with man's natural way," these are unavoidable; however, "as worldly pleasure and the pain of desire originate from man's selfishness," these should be avoided as much as possible. The man admonished that since pain is latent in it, worldly pleasure is not real pleasure.[104] Joken said in answer that he preferred worldly pleasure. However, to the reader, the argument for real pleasure seems stronger. Joken may be said to have expounded hedonism in a reserved manner.

In contrast to Joken, Shiba Kōkan plainly denied the value of honest poverty and advocated pleasure seeking. In an article in the *Scribbles of Shunpa-rō* entitled "On Wealth and Poverty" he said, "Although Yen Hui found pleasure in resting with his head on his elbow, to my mind it is uncomfortable and inconvenient."[105]

The hedonism advocated by Kōkan, however, is not so positive and mundane as that of Norinaga. Rather, it originates from his unique view of adaptation to nature. And the negative happiness and reserved hedonism derived from this adaptation to nature seem, after all, to be characteristic of the psychology of the Japanese.

For instance, in the same work Kōkan expounded, "Don't go to excess but follow the mean." He said that "the true Way is to realize that life is nothing but the vacuity of nature and to die in comfort," and concluded, "Be fully aware that what you cannot do you cannot do. Earn money if you can. Gain fame if you can. Be aware of your limits and don't do what is beyond them."[106] This is Kōkan's view of life, a reshuffle of the principle of the mean, which is rooted in the vacuity of nature, along with hedonism. He was influenced by the Buddhist notion of impermanency embodied in *Essays in Idleness,* Christian cosmology, and European rationalism and he attempted to interpret man's life in terms of the fact "that man and nature were born out of the vacuity of the universe and return to the essential vacuity." He felt that since both Buddhism and Christianity are

104. Ibid.
105. Shiba Kōkan, *Shunpa-rō hikki* [The Scribbles of Shunpa-rō] (1811).
106. Ibid.

heresies, ordinary men should not study them. And he admonished that "when a man at the prime of life studies them, he will become a useless being in the universe."[107] Yet he approved of a man over sixty studying any teaching. Taking his age into consideration, Kōkan seems to have been hinting that he himself would adopt those teachings.

He wrote in the "Records of Kōkan's Regrets" in the *Scribbles of Shunpa-rō* that he was engrossed in the idea "of handing down my name to posterity. . . . After seventy and more years, I have for the first time realized the error I made in the prime of my life. . . . Although one's name is said to be conveyed for a thousand years, it will not be transmitted for one hundred thousand years. In the face of this fact I ponder that one's name is only for one's lifetime." According to Kōkan, "This world is in the midst of the confusion of a dream"; therefore, "while living in this world, I must try not to dream an awesome dream but to live a tranquil life. . . . Sleeping is pleasure; upon awakening, I dream about hell. To keep on sleeping, this is what I call paradise."[108] This is Kōkan's negative hedonism.

What Kōkan called "nature" in the phrase "the vacuity of nature" meant not only the natural surroundings of a human being but also the system in which a human being is a component, with human psychology and conduct all subject to the law of nature. From this view, the incorporation of the individual into nature and the discovery of nature in the individual, there arises a view of adaptation to nature, that is, that the most reasonable way for man to live is to bring himself into accordance with the law of nature.

Even today this view is often cited by many people in their own philosophies of life. Matsunaga Yasuzaemon is a representative example. According to him, "There exists an unmovable and dominant principle behind human life. That is the law of nature. When

---

107. Ibid.
108. Ibid.

rain falls, the soil becomes moistened. This calls to mind the corol-
laries in human life. . . . Our conduct . . . should not go too far. . . .
It is important to walk the path of the mean in accordance with the
law of nature."[109]

Up to this point, Matsunaga's way of thinking does not contradict
the mandate of Heaven and the view of the mean in Confucianism.
In his case, however, nature is superseded by "nature" in the human
being or what he calls "instinct," and he creates a view of life com-
bining a unique adaptation to nature with individualism. "To live
in the natural surroundings and to make good use of them," he said,
"these become my egoism. . . . This is true with money. By all
means I need money. Because I wanted it badly, I ran a coal mine
and even became a speculator. Any work will do as long as it makes
a profit. . . . I just abide by my nature, acting on instinct and going
my way positively. 'It's antisocial'—such an admonition does not
apply to me. . . . The essential point is not to act against human
instinct but to act freely."[110]

Matsunaga's phrase, "as long as it makes a profit," resemble
Kōkan's words, "Earn money if you can." Matsunaga may have
read Kōkan. In any case, Matsunaga replaced the word "nature"
with "instinct," which is natural in a human being, and expounded a
view of life based on instinctivism which is quite far from the con-
ventional Japanese view of life.

For all that, the hedonism of Japan, unlike western hedonism,
springs from emphasizing the negative and directing attention to
the satisfaction of one's wants, setting the Kōkan-style "nature" or
"mean" as one of the starting points and adapting to it. This attitude
is, after all, not free from a reserved and self-conscious attempt to
feel happy.

The attitude of Sakaguchi Ango, who wrote *On Corruption* after
the war and advocated hedonism, strongly contrasts with this atti-

---

109. Matsunaga Yasuzaemon, *Yūki aru jiyū* [A Courageous Freedom] (Tokyo:
     Kaname Shobō, 1953).
110. Ibid.

tude. Taking his departure from the criticism of imperfectionism, he eulogized a hedonism much more positive than Matsunaga's.

Sakaguchi begins with a severe criticism of the hardships which were forced upon the people during the war in the name of a "spirit of austerity." He says in anger, "A virtue of the farming village is said to be the spirit of austerity and endurance. Why is it a virtue to bear austerity?" And he abhors honest poverty, frugality, and modesty, regarding them not as virtues but vices. He also takes the defeat as a matter of course, for "the Japanese soldiers who bore hardships and privation were defeated by the American soldiers who were unable to do so," and he regards the defeat as the rout of the Japanese spirit itself.[111]

Upon the defeat of this belief in insufficiency, there arose a view that "the proper state of the human being and human nature" is "to wish plainly for what one really desires and to reject what one really abhors." This happens because the "love of beauty and pleasure is natural to man, . . . it is the real nature of all men and is nothing to be despised." Sakaguchi insists upon "restoring a true human being from his corruption by 'sound morality' " and "starting on the true birth of oneself and one's nature." For that reason, "Japan and the Japanese ought to be corrupted."[112]

The "corruption" advocated by Sakaguchi, however, differs from decadence in that it is, to a large extent, derived from his latent Buddhist theory. His words, "my corruption to the very end of corruption to find and save myself,"[113] are related to Shinran's words in *A Tract Deploring Heresies of Faith*, "But because I am absolutely incapable of any religious practice, hell is definitely my place."[114] However, there is more to it than that. To Sakaguchi, "although

---

111. Sakaguchi Ango, "Daraku ron" ["On Corruption"], *Shinchō* 43, no. 4 (1946).

112. Ibid.

113. Ibid.

114. Shinran, *Tannishō* [A Tract Deploring Heresies of Faith] (Kyoto: Higashi Honganji, 1961), p. 4.

corruption itself is always a trifle and a vice, there solemnly exists, as one of the characteristics of corruption, solitude, which is the great, true noumenon of a human being. That is, corruption is always solitary and it dooms me to be cast off by others and even by my own parents, and there is no way but to rely solely upon myself."[115] To look upon solitude as the true noumenon of human existence is tantamount to egoism, and it is the realization that there is no way but to rely solely upon oneself.

When these passages are compared with the sense of solitude described by Kōkan, there is an interesting connection between them: "The universe has no beginning. In the ceaseless flow of time men were born. In the ceaseless flow of time men will be born in great numbers. Among them, a being called 'I' is only I, myself. Even parents and brothers are all different beings."[116]

Sakaguchi finds a solitary self in corruption and, owing to the fact that he has no other way, he relies solely upon himself and heads in the direction of strengthening his ego. An effort to find one's self in some guise, to protect it, and to strengthen it is entirely different from what Kōkan called the self of the mean. The fountainhead of Sakaguchi's ideas can be attributed to the extraordinary conditions of postwar Japan.

Sakaguchi's hedonism, revealed in *On Corruption*, rests upon a nonsocial psychological foundation of corruption or solitude characteristic of the postwar society. In comparison with this, a recently published book on successful living entitled *How to Live Life Smartly Henceforth* is probably the first book in Japan on self-cultivation which is based on hedonism. This can be construed from the blurb on the band attached to the cover of the book: "For your success and happiness. . . . There is no harm in admitting today that it is not true that obeying moral laws makes one happy. In fact, though there still are various admonishments using such terms as 'distress'

115. Sakaguchi, *On Corruption*.
116. Shiba, *Scribbles*.

and 'Ten Commandments,' there should not be a happiness in which one's instinct is restrained." With a similar opening passage, the author defines the purpose of human life as hedonistic, materially blessed living. He says, "A man does not live for work. He toils and plays for the purpose of doing a good job, making a success, living a comfortable life, living pleasantly, receiving blessings, and winning success, that is, satisfying himself."[117]

He says that happiness, the aim of human life, is found in amusement, and to work for amusement is the true goal of life. He expounds a philosophy of life based on amusement and affirms that "it is amusement which is the manifestation of what is called happiness.... Human life is only lit up with a fire called amusement."[118]

He then explains why amusement is the truth of the human being: "It is a proven fact that when a man loses his interest in amusement, first his mental functions are enervated, then his mind becomes enfeebled, and finally his body is impaired."[119]

Although this logic is somewhat faulty, this book openly advocating hedonism is probably the only one in postwar Japan to adopt an American attitude toward happiness. In Japan, imperfectionism is still prevalent, so much so that a plain wish for happiness is considered a selfish vice.

---

117. Yoshii Akira, *Korekara no jōzu na ikikata* [How to Live Life Smartly Henceforth] (Tokyo: Bungadō, 1952).
118. Ibid.
119. Ibid.

4. Irrationalism and Rationalism

Our Fate Is in Heaven's Hands

The words "natural reason" and "natural law," which the Japanese often use, imply that human beings are controlled by something irrational, something which denies reason and law. This idea is expressed by such words as the "Way of Heaven, "Heaven's decree," "fate," and "predestination," and it implies control by the hand of an absolute being beyond the cognizance of human wisdom.

There is hardly another people as technologically advanced as the Japanese who attempt to explain social and human affairs using the words "fate" or "destiny." Throughout history many ways of thinking of human affairs and Heaven's decree have been promulgated. The powerful, directly or indirectly, have adopted them as ideological weapons to uphold their power and to regulate the masses.

This Japanese fatalism is divided into two types, fatalism in the narrow sense and predestinarianism. Since fatalism regards all events as a turn of the wheel of fortune or fate, and predestinarianism sees human life as predetermined, both can be related to such notions as previous life and future life, karma, and cause and effect. Both ideas are included in the words, *tendō* (the Way of Heaven) and *tenmei* (Heaven's decree), which are sometimes used interchangeably.

Fatalism of either type was used by the powerful in feudal society as an important ideological weapon, and the attitude toward Heaven's decree and the Way of Heaven is often expounded in the didactic books on the way of the warrior.

In the text of the 1667 edition of *Refutation and Correction of the Record of Kusunoki Hyōgo* fate is classified in detail and explained as follows:

If a warrior does not classify fate, he is not a warrior. There are five fates: the fate of Heaven, the fate of man, the fate of the world, fate of affairs, and the fate of reason. If, despite the fact that a sage governs a country, it is visited by a natural calamity such as flood or drought, or if, even though the master of the country is an evil ruler, he lives to a great age, these are what is called the fate of Heaven. If a ruler of eminent virtue flourishes and a vicious ruler declines, this is what is called the fate of man. If one has not done wrong, yet is ruined because of the vicissitudes of the world, this is what is called the fate of the world. If one makes inevitable mistakes and ruins oneself, this is what is called the fate of affairs. . . . If, because of a predestined reason, one's ups and downs all accord with reason, this is what is called the fate of reason.[1]

After this comprehensible classification, the author in the end advocates fatalism, saying, "Nothing could be beyond the five fates."

In the case of warriors, however, he looks upon "those who leave themselves to the fate of Heaven and never think of virtue and vice as fools," and he admonishes, "those who strive for bravery should have regard not for the fate of Heaven but for the fate of man, for setting a value on the fate of Heaven is almost a vice."[2] This is a conditioned fatalism. It does not include submitting oneself completely to the fate of Heaven, for there still remains the positive ability to shift man's fate by human strength.

In connection with this idea, in the fatalism of the way of the warrior, the relation between the rise and fall of man and morality is considered in the *Hagakure*: "The virtue and vice of a man should not be judged by his rise or decline. Rise and decline are matters of Heaven. Virtue and vice are matters of man."[3] In other words, the

---

1. Ejima Tamenobu, *Ketsogi Hyōgoki* [Refutation and Correction of the Record of Kusunoki Hyōgo] (1667).
2. Ibid.
3. Yamamoto Jinemon Jōchō, *Hagakure* [In the Shade of Leaves] (1716).

vicissitudes of life are subject to the heavenly and natural law and are beyond human control; virtue and vice, however, as the way of man, are regulated by another law, different from the Way of Heaven. The fate of man seems to be similar in content to this way of man.

In the case of warriors, however, predestinarianism, the belief that social status and class are predestined by Heaven's decree, is emphasized. In *Precepts for Warring Men* Heaven is emphasized as the basis for knowing contentment and comfort: "Since wealth and nobility are in the hands of Heaven, it is hard to seek after them. Inasmuch as reading books and governing oneself are in the hands of man, these are easy to do. Instead of tormenting oneself in the quest for things hard to acquire, one should set one's mind at ease with things easily acquired."[4]

However, in regard to the prevalence of injustice in the world and the prosperity of the wicked, one can hardly take them only as the fate of Heaven and Heaven's decree. Therefore, many attempts are made to explain this injustice. For example, Ekiken said in *Instructions for Beginners*, "There are men who, despite their accumulation of merit, are not blessed. It is because they were born extremely unblessed in fortune and luck. There are also men who, though they commit wrongdoings, bring about no disaster. It is because they were born with ample vitality and favored by fortune." Owing to this inequality in fortune and luck, one may suffer injustice. However, the notion of retribution enters in: "If one is not recompensed in one's lifetime, one's offspring will certainly be rewarded. . . . It is the law of nature that good and evil are always accompanied by their fitting retribution. Never doubt it! Also, one is endowed with fortune and misfortune. This is Heaven's decree."[5]

Ekiken called one's innate fortune or misfortune Heaven's decree and, in contrast to this, he called retribution for good or evil *tenri*, the rule of Heaven. The injustice of Heaven's decree is thus com-

---

4. Izawa Nagahide, *Shoshi danshikun* [Precepts for Warring Men] (1717).
5. Kaibara Ekiken, *Shogakukun* [Instructions for Beginners] (1718).

pensated for by the rule of Heaven. The word *tenri* signifies predestination, corresponding to such terms as "cause and effect" or "karma."

In contrast, *mei* (destiny) and *unmei* (fate) as used by Nakae Tōju
are much more predestinarian, in that he looked upon everything in
terms of prearrangement by destiny. He says, in *Old Men's Dialogue*,
"Every situation one is placed in during one's lifetime, good and ill
luck, fortune and misfortune, even a drink and a meal, is subject to
destiny. . . . One's being fortunate enough to be wealthy and noble
has been predestined, and nothing is the fruit of one's own effort.
One's being unfortunate enough to be poor and humble has been
predestined. It is neither the fault of parents nor the work of man nor
the error of the Way of Heaven."[6]

Tōju goes on to explain that since the functions of the cosmic dual
forces and the five natural elements and "even the influence of retribution for good and evil are intermingled during one's growth
in the womb for ten [lunar] months": the fate of one's life "does not
follow a course that allows one to be born with only the good parts
of fate."[7] This is the logic of divination and is the most complicated
fatalism.

In Japan views on fate emerged repeatedly in the form of elab-
orate arguments among the classical intellectuals. In sermons for
merchants and peasants, those below the rank of warrior, fatalism
has been effectively used as a justification for the concept of knowing
contentment and comfort.

First of all, since one's trade or occupation is bestowed as a token
of Heaven's decree, turning one's back on it is as bad as disobeying
the decree. The *shingaku* book by Tejima Toan, *The General Idea of the
Shingaku Fellowship*, is a good example. It reads: "Not of his own will
is a man born in a family and succeeds to its trade, whatever it may
be, agriculture, industry, or commerce. Because his trade is acquired
by happy chance, it should be taken as Heaven's decree. Therefore,

---

6. Nakae Tōju, *Okina mondō* [Old Men's Dialogue] (1866).
7. Ibid.

his neglecting it even to the slightest extent means he is going against Heaven's decree and committing a great crime."[8]

In the case of warriors, something similar to the fate of man is suggested, contrary to Heaven's decree. However, in the case of townsmen, words such as "going against Heaven's decree is a great crime" were used. This menacing manner becomes increasingly conspicuous in directives to peasants. *Instructions for the Farming Household*, which presents directions for farmers on their conduct in life, clearly says that human beings innately possess a portion of Heaven's decree; therefore, "there will be neither regret nor wish if we intimidate peasants, saying, 'Being a peasant is by Heaven's decree. Being poor and humble is by Heaven's decree.' "[9] These words aptly sum up the political significance of fatalism.

By means of a similar threat based on the view of Heaven's decree, resignation was infused into women. In the *Sequel to the Sequel to Kyūō's Moral Discourses* the lot of a wife is said to be destined by Heaven's decree. "After coming to her husband's home, whether the wife undergoes many hardships or secures an enviable position is attributed to Heaven's decree. . . . There is no way out even if she wants to flee from such circumstances. . . . One out of a hundred wives discards her husband and returns to the home of her parents. She is married again to another man and she may get a better life. However, this woman will surely encounter times when her mind, though she is living a desirable life, will be tormented. If she obeys her husband and abides by the Way, she may suffer outwardly but inwardly she is at ease."[10] The retribution for acting contrary to Heaven's decree is said to be a troubled mind. In other words, "Inasmuch as human beings inherit a nature of benevolence and

---

8. Tejima Toan, *Kaiyū taishi* [The General Idea of the *Shingaku* Fellowship] (1773).
9. Tanaka Kyūgū, *Minka bunryōki* [Instructions for the Farming Household] (1721).
10. Kyūō, *Zoku zoku Kyūō dōwa* [Sequel to the Sequel to Kyūō's Moral Discourses] (1835).

justice, they feel uneasy when they force their way even to a slight degree. This is what I call the living decree of Heaven."[11] A troubled mind corresponds to qualms of conscience. This approach looks more appealing after inner reflection than the simple doctrine of heavenly punishment.

The view of Heaven's decree further develops into a very convenient excuse that since "reward is originally an aid of Heaven, it is impossible for human intent to change it. . . . Punishment is to be cast off by Heaven by one's own choice. . . . Punishment is naturally imposed by surprise. This is called *myōga* [divine providence]."[12] In brief, unhappiness is the outcome of human behavior, corresponding to punishment, whereas happiness is regulated by the Way of Heaven and is beyond human control. In the Japanese language, happiness is expressed by such words as *shiawase*, good fortune, or *kōun*, good luck. This is undoubtedly a vestige of the philosophy that sees happiness as beyond human power, a boon from Heaven. Proverbs such as "Sleep and wait till the wheel of fortune turns your way," "Everything comes to those who wait," and "Things will just happen to your satisfaction" arose from such a philosophy.

This way of thinking, on one hand, leads to the principle of adaptation of nature. The *Sequel to Kyūō's Moral Discourses* reads that the purport of *shingaku* is to attain the state of mind at which this principle aims. "A yawn, a sneeze, and a finger motion, none can be properly done unless the right time comes. . . . To know what can be done and what cannot be done makes one greatly relieved."[13]

The resignation of the Japanese is to be aware of this decree of Heaven and to be at ease; it differs markedly from the despair of the West. Despair is not the resignation demanded by the Way of Heaven but is the "unreasonable suffering of a man who takes impossible things to be possible." The acceptance of Heaven's decree does not mean to despair as the result of attachment but is, from the

---

11. Ibid.

12. Seki Ichiraku, *Myōgakun* [Precepts of Divine Providence] (1724).

13. Kyūō, *Zoku Kyūō dōwa* [Sequel to Kyūō's Moral Discourses] (1835).

outset, to resign oneself detachedly and decisively. This is what is called adaptation to nature.

Resignation to Heaven's decree does not mean that no effort is necessary, but that the relation between the power of fate and the power of man is seen from a different angle, as stated in the proverb "Do your best and leave the rest to Providence." In accordance with the differences in allocation of these two powers, the stamp of the fatalist or realist is determined.

In the works of Saikaku fate and fortune are viewed as inevitability and resourcefulness. He, on one hand, describes predestinarianism thus: "Man's fate is all in Heaven's hand. . . . Death is predestined in one's previous life."[14] On the other hand, he says, "It is hard to be a man of wealth unless one's resourcefulness is assisted by fortune."[15] What he is trying to say is that *bungen* (one's place in life) is determined by the proportion of fate to resourcefulness.

There Is Always a Way Out of Difficulty

Belief in Heaven's decree is, even now, one of the indispensable items in any book of conduct. Let me quote just one sample from a book entitled *Passivity and Life* as an example of the same time-worn logic translated into contemporary language. "In fine, poverty and fortune are gifts of the gods. . . . However, no matter how long you wait, you may not be blessed. If so, you must be resigned and take it as Heaven's decree and never doubt it."[16]

As long as one believes in Heaven's decree, it is necessary for one to have an attitude of passivity in conformity with the principle of

---

14. Ihara Saikaku, *Yono hitogokoro* [Human Sentiments of the World] (1694).
15. Ihara Saikaku, *Nihon eitaigura* [The Eternal Storehouse of Japan] (1688).
16. Tamura Reishō, *Omakase to jinsei* [Passivity and Life] (Tokyo: Tenshindō-honbu, 1942).

adaptation to nature. "Taking misfortune as misfortune, you must leave anything and everything to the gods."[17]

What is more suitable for intellectuals than the question of passivity is the distinction between absolute fate and relative fate mentioned by Ebara Koyata in his book, *The Place Where Your Mind Should Be*, which is a view close to the fate of heaven and fate of man mentioned earlier. According to him, "There are two fates, absolute fate and relative fate. Absolute fate is beyond the power of man; however, relative fate may be changed by one's strength. Therefore, the so-called decree of Heaven corresponds to this absolute fate."[18]

Relative fate can be controlled by religious prayers. However, with absolute fate it would not do any good to cling to gods and buddhas. "Relative fate may come under the law of cause and effect, that is, a good cause for a good effect and a bad cause for a bad effect. On the contrary, absolute fate may bring a good cause for a bad effect or a bad cause for a good effect."[19] If fate is so divided, absolute fate is responsible for the unhappiness in life and relative fate for happiness as a result of one's prayers to gods and buddhas. It is a natural solution for Ebara, whose logic expounds a Buddhist philosophy of life.

Ebara also expresses awareness of the principle of adaptation to nature based upon Buddhism by using the phrase, "I leave myself to you." In terms of the union of Heaven's decree and human affairs, he says, "I leave all my affairs to the discretion of Amita Buddha and work diligently, submitting myself to fate. . . . Therein lies the state of 'leaving myself to you' in which absolute fate and relative fate become concordant."[20]

However, passivity has penetrated the psychology of the Japanese not only in the form of Buddhist resignation or self-cultivation. In

---

17. Ibid.
18. Ebara Koyata, *Kokoro no okidokoro* [The Place Where Your Mind Should Be] (Tokyo: Kōfūkan, 1951).
19. Ibid.
20. Ibid.

many cases, even among intellectuals and petite bourgeoisie, who are both considered to be enlightened, the acceptance of the decree of Heaven lurks somewhere in the mind under various guises.

A woman depicted in *A Woman Who Washes the Loincloth of a Green Ogre*, written by Sakaguchi Ango, is representative of this view of adaptation to nature. Her rambling reminiscences are quite interesting. "There is somehow a way out of difficulty; this is the philosophy of life which I have learned so far." This woman describes her state of mind during the war: "Although the newspapers and radio were proclaiming the crisis, and rumors in the streets were whispering the decline of Japan, I did not care about the future of Japan because I was able to believe in my own survival. I had confidence, like a stiffness of mind, that there would always be a way out in time of difficulty."[21] These words are an accurate reflection of the petty Japanese citizen's selfish adaptation to nature.

To the majority of the Japanese masses after the war ended it seemed futile to think of such concepts as "fatherland" and "race" which were felt to "be too lofty and empty." This is unfortunately still true. Therefore, when difficulties come, they do not try to solve the difficulties themselves but say, "It will turn out well naturally." The word "naturally" means according to the forces of the traditional heaven and destiny. Belief in heaven's decree results in a philosophy which disregards the future of Japan as long as the individual's own life turns out well.

This, too, is not despair but a sort of indolence derived from Japanese resignation. In this respect, the attitude can be viewed not as dismal despair but as ignorant optimism. A prostitute wrote in her memoirs: "If those so-and-sos [American soldiers] would return to their homes, there would be no unfortunate women. I hope they will go home soon. If the so-and-sos go home, I too will quit working as a dancer. It's inevitable, for everything in this world submits

---

21. Sakaguchi Ango, *Ao-oni no fundoshi o arau onna* [A Woman Who Washes the Loincloth of a Green Ogre] (Tokyo: Yamane Shoten, 1947).

to fate. It's foolish to think, isn't it?"[22] From fatalism to passivity to thoughtlessness—the path is clear.

This postwar fatalism obviously also sprang from a psychology which saw the defeat as one of Heaven's decrees. That is, "How was the war going to turn out? No doubt Japan would be defeated, the Americans would land on the mainland, and the greater part of the Japanese people would be annihilated. But all this could be conceived of only as part of a supernatural destiny, the decree of Heaven, so to speak."[23]

The intensification of postwar fatalism, of course, should not be attributed only to the fact that the end of the war came in the shape of an awesome natural calamity caused by "supernatural" atomic bombs. The Japanese people, who had suffered under irrational fascists and a long war, were more or less bound to become fatalists.

Since the military men in Japan had always depended on the grace of Heaven and divine intervention to continue the war rather than on rational and scientific calculations, it was a matter of course that fatalism was absorbed unconsciously by all members of the military, from the top to the bottom.

In 1943, in the midst of the war, Lieutenant General Nakai Ryō-tarō positively stated in his *On Generals*, "It is a fact that victory or defeat in warfare is ascribable to something transcending logic, namely, fate or the grace of Heaven. Moreover, this has been true throughout history." Reflecting upon his war experiences, he testified that this fatalism is increasingly intensified in time of war. "I presume there is hardly a commander who, being responsible for many lives, does not fall into the idea of doing his best first, then praying for the grace of Heaven and divine intervention. Especially

---

22. Takenaka Katsuo, *Gaishō* [Streetgirls—Actual Conditions and Their Memoirs] (Tokyo: Yūkōsha, 1949).

23. Sakaguchi Ango, "Hakuchi" ["The Idiot"], George Saito, trans., in *Modern Japanese Stories, An Anthology*, Ivan I. Morris, ed. (Tokyo: Charles E. Tuttle Co., 1961), p. 125.

at the time of an operation, his faith becomes more and more firm."[24]

In Japanese military education, resignation based upon fatalism was regarded as a sort of brave determination and labeled "detachment," and the spirit of unrecognized service was cherished. In the military, "Detachment is emphasized. . . . For instance, it is improper to wish for honor on the battlefield. Everyone must attain an attitude of readiness to be a weed-covered corpse, a man whose identity is unknown in death, or to die suddenly in an airplane somewhere in the sky, unrecognized."[25]

Scattered through the memoirs of students who died in action are the pitiful words of those who, facing death, attempted to calm their minds by thinking of fate and predestiny. "As one of the men who were born into this world . . . let us shoulder our innate fate, work up to our capacity as individually destined, and fight with all our might. . . . It is cowardly of us to turn our backs on the destined way, giving trifling reasons. Let us follow the destined way and fight it out as Heaven orders us."[26]

Life Is Hard

Not only soldiers on the battle lines but also many of the citizens were bound to fall into a state of mind that accepted the war as a sort of fate. Dazai Osamu delineates this psychology in his short autobiographical essay. "Despite the fact that there wasn't even one article which seemed believable throughout the entire war in Japanese newspapers, we tried to force ourselves to believe them and be ready to die. If a parent were on the verge of bankruptcy and told a

---

24. Nakai Ryōtarō, *Shōsuiron* [On Generals] (Tokyo: Daiyamondo Sha, 1943).

25. Iizuka Kōji, *Nihon no guntai* [The Japanese Military] (Tokyo: Tokyo Daigaku Shuppanbu, 1950).

26. Committee for Compiling Notes of Student Soldiers Killed in World War II, eds., *Haruka naru yamakawani* [To Far-off Mountains and Rivers] (Tokyo: Mikasa Shobō, 1952).

transparent and painful lie, would it be possible for a child to expose the secret? All the child could do would be to die silently with his parent, submitting to fate."[27]

The fatalism of the Japanese has, after all, a great psychological effect, for it provides a psychological safeguard against unhappiness. It is the cultivation of a constant habit of resignation, taking everything as fate and predestination.

In the mass entertainment of Japan, especially in popular songs and *rōkyoku* chants, the words "fate," "predestination," and "destiny" frequently appear. It seems as if the masses spontaneously receive an education in fatalism by seeing, uttering, or listening to these words everyday. Conversely, since fatalism is firmly rooted in the minds of the masses, stories and songs using those words are in demand, and such works have a high commodity value. By this circuit of intensification, fatalism has not declined but has grown in proportion to the bleakness of the prospects of the world.

Several popular songs are good examples of this:

How sad, the fate of red shoes!
The paths are two but you are alone.
Even the shoestrings are torn off with tears.
Good-bye, good-bye.
   Ah, the flowers scatter at the distant whistle!
      "Tango of Red Shoes"

Parted at the dark wharf,
   weep for the bitter fate;
Ah, how painful the tears
   shed in the foggy night in Shanghai.
I'm here, your Riru,
   as I was on that night.
I'm Riru, sad Riru.
      "I'm Riru"

---

27. Dazai Osamu, "Jūgo nenkan" ["For Fifteen Years"], *Bunka Tenbō* 4 (1946).

You sailed across the seas
   all alone;
Don't cast away your hope, Riru,
Riru, Riru, who came back from Shanghai.
Let us share our dismal fate
   and live together
   as we used to.
Riru, Riru,
I can't find you, Riru, not even today.
Is there anyone
   who knows where Riru is?
        "Riru Who Came Back From Shanghai"

Furthermore, there are many songs similar to the following one which encourages resignation to fate.

My nature is that of a bird
   so I leave everything to song.
Even love and tears
   I leave to song.
Don't sulk,
   don't turn sulky,
   for it is fate.
        "A Street Singer in Izu"

As is clear in these examples, fate is symbolized by dismal, sad, and painful parting. The fact that the verbs used overwhelmingly in Japanese popular songs are "weep" and "part," followed by "resign" and "float," is evidence of the frequent use of a theme of fatalism and impermanency.

In *rōkyoku* chants, fate or destiny is often the subject.

However painful and trying,
We must bear
   even what makes our hearts bleed.
. . . .

This is our fate,
   we who ought to live.
      "Akagi Lullaby"

A long-lasting fight
   in the floating world,
Victory or defeat,
   all is up to fate.
Don't worry,
   we will win again
   when the time comes.
      "A Town of Lordless Samurai"

Why Do I Have Such Bad Fortune?

Fatalism in the *yakuza* world, which *rōkyoku* chants deal with, is
expressed in outmoded words, *inga* (causality) and *innen* (destiny).

What causality makes the two of us,
   who as newborn babies were bathed in the same stream,
   compete against each other for ten years?
It's man's persistence and emulation.
      "Tempō *Yakuza* Story"

What kind of destiny is this?
I nursed the wife of a man
   whom I had killed.
      "The *Yakuza*'s Back Road"

What has caused me to become a *yakuza*?
I live a life of fighting and gambling.
While living under the *yakuza* code of morals
   and making a living by dice,
I, at last, fell into the plight
   of killing my foster father

with my own sword.
   "Akagi Lullaby"

As can be seen in these three examples, destiny brings after all a dismal fate: two friends from childhood become rivals, a *yakuza* nurses the wife of a man whom he has killed, and another *yakuza* kills the uncle who had raised him.

As is expressed in the frequently used phrase, "This is the fate of a *yakuza*," inhuman conditions never found in the society of "decent" people are thought to emerge predeterminedly in the world of the *yakuza*. The conditions which emerge because of their peculiar human relationships, called *jingi* (the *yakuza* code of morals) or *ongi* (a debt of gratitude), are attributed to a supernatural fate, wherein the tragic sensation is intensified and the feeling of guilt diluted. Killing unknown men in a fight over a *yakuza*'s territory is expressed in these terms: "This is the fate of a *yakuza*—I killed men against whom I had no grudge and fled to join others." The *yakuza* somehow comes to be seen as innocent; he is sympathized with as something pitiful and transient, ruled by fate.

Needless to say, this doctrine of causality has long been diffused widely among the Japanese masses through the medium of Buddhism. In Hakuin's Buddhist hymns, this karmic retribution is continually preached. "All who were born in this world, the noble and the humble, the poor and the rich alike, wish for good health, longevity, and money. Why then are we doomed to suffer from ill health, early death, and poverty? It is because the seeds we sowed in the previous life are growing in this life."[28]

In *shingaku*, too, the idea of retribution is likewise the undercurrent of the morality expounded. However, the ideas expressed in *shingaku* are more practical precepts than those of Buddhism. According to *shingaku* good conduct and a good attitude bring forth happiness within one's lifetime without fail; it is not a matter of retribution

---

28. Hakuin, *Zenaku tanemaki kagami wasan* [Buddhist Hymn Mirroring the Sowing of Good and Evil] (1835).

in the life after death but during this life. It is said, for example, that if a child is dutiful to his parents, he will be happy after he becomes an adult. "Whatever your parents ask, you must answer 'yes' at once and do willingly what you are told to do. If you do so, you will be blessed when you grow up."[29]

On the other hand, if a child does not fulfill his moral obligation, he will encounter misfortune after he becomes an adult. "What is called retribution is sad and dreadful. . . . Children who learn how to talk big from their infancy . . . will become miserable beings."[30]

Thus, the idea of retribution expounded in *shingaku* is practical and positive, even though it is called "fate," because one's attitude and conduct influence the result. In spite of using the same term, "fatalism," *shingaku* takes a stand which gives more credit to man's effort then does the view based on Buddhist causality or karma.

Fatalism begets varied nuances of philosophy depending on the different weights apportioned to human efforts and to Heaven's decree. There are extreme views of causality and karma: anything and everything is prearranged by karma; no matter how hard a man tries or how much merit he accumulates, the result is bad; it was inevitable.

The philosophy of karma has been utilized more or less as the most effective basis for resignation by all Japanese religions, ranging from Buddhism to the popular religions. The following quote is a sample of the contemporary view of predestination borrowed from the philosophy of karma in Buddhism. "The program of man's life has been prearranged from beginning to end. . . . You must realize that worry for the future is utterly useless." Then, "what we are doing now becomes the cause . . . and has a bearing on what happens ten or twenty years ahead and even in the life after death"; therefore, "no juggling of life is possible."[31] In view of the fact that the present life affects the future, self-cultivation becomes momentous. In this

29. Tejima Toan, *Kukyō* [Teachings on the Manner of Speaking] (1773).
30. Ibid.
31. Tamura, *Passivity and Life.*

respect, this karmic philosophy is identical with the reasoning of *shingaku*.

In the teaching of Tenrikyō, which is still influential as a folk religion, causation is said to be the revelation of providence and is looked upon as the result of *hokori* (dust) accumulated in the past. This "dust" is divided into the eight "dusts" or cravings of man, miserliness, covetousness, hatred, self-love, enmity, anger, avarice, and arrogance. There are altogether ten bad habits of mind, for God the Parent said, "I don't like lying and flattery."

The result of the "dust" accumulated during this life is causation from this life, and the "dust" accumulated in repeated metempsychoses is causation from previous lives. Therefore, one's encountering diverse mishaps is the result of the heap of "dust" which is bestowed by God the Parent as a warning.

Tenrikyō explains unhappiness as heavenly punishment of varying intensity and divides it into several degrees in proportion to the anger of God the Parent. In *The Essentials of Tenrikyō* published after the war, there are such items as *"Innen"* (heavenly cause and effect) and *"Hokori"* (dust) in the chapter entitled "Outline of Teachings," and we read the following: "We call sickness and invalidism *mijō* (personal condition) and uncontrollable difficulties and disasters *jijō* (natural disaster). God the Parent, by means of manifestations of all the *hokori* as *mijō* and *jijō*, wishes to cleanse man's mind and to actualize His ideal, a joyous life full of merriment for all." The joyous life described here is the ideal life of Tenrikyō, which means to live "with *seiten no kokoro* (mind of a clear sky), no matter what difficulty and disaster one comes across, taking them thankfully, gratefully, and willingly. . . . The warning of God the Parent pertaining to *hokori* is bestowed first in the form of *tebiki* (divine guidance) and *michi ose* (divine direction). If it is still not recognized, it gradually becomes more obvious beginning with *iken* (remonstrance) and going on to *zannen* (vexation) and *rippuku* (wrath)."[32]

---

32. Ikoma Fujio, *Tenrikyō yogi* [The Essentials of *Tenrikyō*] (Tanbaichi-cho, Nara Ken: Tenrikyo Jihōsha, 1948).

The charm of Tenrikyō lies in its blessing in this life and in the brightness and positivity of a joyous life. "Pain, agony, swellings, fever, and loose bowels, all is dust in your mind," thus reads the *Ofudesaki* (Book of Revelation). This is not negative resignation, for one takes "*mijō* and *jijō* as flowers along the Way," and "resolves to overcome them spiritedly."[33]

In Tenrikyō, a shift is made from a view of absolutism based on Heaven's decree to a notion of relative fate, that is, fate that can be overcome by human effort. One is therefore urged neither to submit to unhappiness, taking it as *innen*, nor to become desperate; rather, one should live through the fate. "There is no way out, for to be or not to be is all presided over by *innen*. If it is said, then there is no way out"; therefore, "we must live through it at all costs."[34]

Acts of *zange* (repentance) should be performed to sweep away *hokori* and "purify" *innen*. "Repentance for the *innen* of previous lives" is called *tannō* (the spirit of contentment). *Tannō* is not resignation but helps one "to advance positively along the path of purification of *innen*. . . . Inasmuch as *tannō* results in blossoms of joy, it accords with reason."[35]

Whether following Tenrikyō or another belief, the idea of causality and karma comes to be linked with the recognition that one's life is a loan from God, a charge. In Tenrikyō, this is explained as follows: "Anyway, man's body is 'a loan' and 'only his mind is his own.' Since his body is 'a loan,' he must someday return it to its lender, God the Parent. The time of restitution . . . is not called 'death' but *denaoshi* (departure for rebirth). God the Parent teaches us, 'It is not dying but like exchanging an old cloth for a new one.' "[36] Therefore, a man should not regard his life as his own possession. It is beyond "human speculation, . . . a thing which individ-

---

33. Ibid.
34. Ibid.
35. Ibid.
36. Ibid.

ual minds cannot set to work,"[37] for God the Parent freely makes it work.

Predestinarianism, in which one thinks of oneself in terms of a loan or a charge from God becomes psychological grounds for the spirit of service above self.

A student in a suicide unit wrote the following letter to his mother: "Please be cautious of making any indecent grumble; say that since their lives are but borrowed from His Majesty, they have to offer them for the sake of His Majesty."[38] Resignation is thus forced upon the mother, who must regard even her son's life as a loan from His Majesty: to offer it is obligatory. In this example the piteous state of the people, who in the name of predestination could not even shed tears when they were suffering, is obvious.

On one hand, this view of predestination, in which a human life is regarded as a gift of God, has been negatively called absolute resignation. On the other hand, as seen in the doctrine of Tenrikyō, it resolves into a positive effort to cherish and better the body received as a loan. The relation between Heaven's decree, human affairs, and human strength in each theory determines the final attitude.

Do Your Best and Leave the Rest to Providence

Concerning the equilibrium between Heaven's decree and human strength which I have previously mentioned, the effect of human strength is often described in the older view of Heaven's decree. Especially in the views of the Tokugawa period on Heaven's decree, human effort is, in the last analysis, evaluated higher than absolute predestination in the morality of the warrior, though not in that of

---

37. Ibid.
38. Committee for Compiling Notes, *To Far-off Mountains and Rivers.*

the townsman and peasant. For example, in *Precepts for the Warrior*, it is said that "to be ignorant of worldly affairs and to live in accord with the Way of Heaven is improper. The Way of Heaven is latent within you, not outside. Do your best, then leave the rest to Heaven."[39] This is in contrast to threatening commoners with Heaven's decree. Heaven's decree and man's fate are distinguished as follows: "In spite of the fact that the decree is in Heaven's hands, its achievement is in our hands. Although the decree is in Heaven's hands, it is latent in us. This is called fate. Heaven's decree and man's fate become one."[40] In the case of warriors, man's fate and Heaven's decree stand side by side.

However, Kaibara Ekiken says, in *Instructions for Beginners*, that people in any class can win the fate of Heaven by human strength: "If a warrior serves his lord earnestly, he will be in the lord's favor and will be given a higher stipend. If a farmer cultivates his fields well, his fall harvest will be abundant. If artisans and merchants are diligent in their trades, they will become wealthy."[41]

Ekiken recommends effort as a means to win Heaven's decree on one's own, saying, "Work diligently." However, as seen later, in the case of warriors he says that what affects Heaven's decree is not only service but also the application of principle and reason; in opposition to the irrationality of fatalism, the element of rationality is emphasized.

In contemporary ethics for living, Heaven's decree and human affairs are expounded in a tone similar to Ekiken's. Izumiyama Sanroku, a statesman, says in the preface to *Encyclopedia for the Art of Living*: " The decree comes from Heaven. He who knows Heaven's decree is the top man in life. . . . Each individual does his best in his lot in life. . . . A man who knows Heaven's decree will be able to

---

39. Izawa Nagahide, *Bushikun* [Precepts for the Warrior] (1715).
40. Ibid.
41. Kaibara, *Instructions for Beginners*.

elevate his position and status in life spontaneously."[42] "To do one's best," as used here, has the same meaning as Ekiken's "service"; however, how one should make such an effort is not specified.

A businessman, Ayukawa Gisuke, who has gone through scientific training as a technical expert, cherishes fatalism as his faith. He estimates the equilibrum between man's capability and fate in the following manner: "You talk about loss and gain, but it's chance. It's fate rather than your capacity. Almost ninety-nine percent is fate. No matter how much you think, you cannot do as you plan to do in this world, unless the wheel of fortune turns your way. There is a change in the program. . . . Isn't it fate that, from of old, has been likened to a patch of baldness at the back of one's head? [Just as you cannot grasp the hair of a man who has a bald patch at the back of his head, fate can not be seized and controlled.] In many cases, the choice between success or failure is within the grip of fate, and man has nothing to do with it."[43]

Perhaps fatalism of this sort is latent in the minds of the majority of the Japanese people; in cases of war or emergency it has turned into resignation, enlightenment, or sophistry and has helped to dilute unhappiness.

Therefore, although the Japanese seem to make a design of their life by their own effort and to make headway toward that purpose by using their reasoning, they tend, because of their consideration that human strength lies within the limits of Heaven's decree, to give up when they come to a deadlock, saying, "All is decreed by Heaven." The fact that this tendency is regarded as a virtue, with such modifiers as "resigned," "manly," and "detached," stems from the Japanese psychology whose counterpart is not found in any other contemporary country. In brief, the brittleness and lack of tenacity resulting from a weakness of self are apt to be charged to Heaven's

---

42. Ōyama Hiromichi, *Shosei hyakka jiten* [Encyclopedia for the Art of Living] (Tokyo: Saginomiya Shobō, 1951).

43. Ayukawa Gisuke in *Watakushi no seikatsu shinjō* [My Belief in Life], ed., Jitsugyō no Nihonsha (Tokyo: Jitsugyō no Nihonsha, 1953).

decree, supplementing a pathetic feeling that one has tried every means possible.

On the other hand, realists who oppose fatalism are called "unresigned," "tenacious," "unsubmissive," "attached," and even "brazen." Praise of persistence is not abundant among the Japanese. Therefore, the following words of Matsunaga Yasuzaemon sound unusual, for he evaluates man's power highly and disparages the view that Heaven's decree is absolute: "Human affairs are endless. . . . I do not see the reasoning of a man who ceases working halfway and says that he has tried every possible means. No work is completed until you die. Whether there is Heaven or decree, human vitality, the power of execution, and the human spirit are independent of such things."[44]

Why did Matsunaga write passages such as this? When he was invited to a tea ceremony at Odawara, the host asked all the guests to write fine expressions in an album. According to Matsunaga, "On the first page of the album, an old Sinologist by the name of Shionoya On skillfully wrote an old maxim, 'Do your best and leave the rest to Providence!' After him . . . I wrote without hesitation, 'I will do what I intend to do. Why should I ask Heaven for help?' . . . I did not like such mushy jargon separating human affairs from Heaven's decree, doing one's best for the sake of an excuse and leaving the rest to God's will."[45]

This episode clearly shows the contrast between a realistic capitalist and a Sinologist with faith in the Oriental view of Heaven's decree.

Things in the World Are Not Always Comprehensible

The fatalism being discussed is a sort of irrationalism which denies

---

44. Matsunaga Yasuzaemon, *Yūki aru jiyū* [A Courageous Freedom] (Tokyo: Kaname Shobō, 1953).
45. Ibid.

the laws of nature and society and looks upon every reality in terms of the domination of superhuman and supernatural forces. This irrationalism is still the basis for the philosophy of life of many Japanese.

Kageyama Masaharu, in talking about the July 5th Incident, told the following story illustrative of this irrationalism: "The senior Maeda attempted to kill himself, pointed a pistol against his head, and pulled the trigger three times, but the shell did not go off. The pistol, which was not a trick pistol, misfired. What else can we ascribe this to but Providence? This point can be measured neither by scientism nor rationalism."[46]

This irrationalism originates in fatalism and is a type of nonscientism in which things are never thought of logically. A formula like "being scientific is being un-Japanese" was warrantable until quite recently. This is obvious in a criticism of scientific thinking made by Sugawara Hyōji, author of *The Way of the Farmer-Warrior*, which was published during the war: "Stop leaning toward such an un-Japanese thing as analysis and theory."[47] In other words, nonscientism and irrationalism are typically Japanese.

As a result, there were many people who thought of the confrontation of the Orient, especially Japan, with the West and concluded that the core of the Japanese way of thinking was the denial of scientism and lack of faith in rationalism. This tendency has decreased since the war. Earlier, however, even among the so-called literati and thinkers of Japan there were some who not only assumed as a matter of course that rationalism would fail to develop in Japan but also saw rationalism as unfit and harmful to the Japanese system of social mores. This is ridiculous, for as I will show later, rationalism has been in existence for some time in various forms in Japan. Japa-

---

46. Kageyama Masaharu, *7.5 Jiken kōhan kiroku* [Records of the Trials of the July 5th Incident] (Tokyo: Daitōjuku Shuppanbu, 1942).
47. Sugawara Hyōji, *Tōyō nōdō no kyogaku* [The Way of the Farmer-Warrior] (Tokyo: Tōe Shoin, 1939).

nese attitudes are not always or necessarily irrational in comparison to western attitudes.

However, when the Japanese spirit was extensively propagandized, there were many intellectuals who believed that the analysis and theory denounced by Sugawara Hyōji was characteristic of the scientism of foreign shores, especially of Europe, and could never be used by the Japanese.

Yokomitsu Riichi in his *Loneliness on a Journey* depicts several types of these antiscientists: "I use the so-called abstract nouns of foreign origin only for the purpose of analysis, but when it is a case of measuring a man's philosophy of life, I am careful to use them as little as possible." Or, "In the past in Japan, while common sense was the standard, logic had not been employed openly; then came the Meiji era when European intellectuality was introduced. Since this intellectuality is the ability to analyze, people began to analyze everything including common sense and feelings. That is characteristic of the Taishō and Shōwa periods."[48]

The Japanists thought European intellectuality and scientism were attempting to analyze man's psychology, reason, and feelings although they are beyond analysis. In other words, the argument was that the laws concerning nature may be tentatively recognized as natural science, yet in regard to society and man analysis is not recommended. If an analysis were forcibly made, it would result in the worship of Europe. "If an analysis is made, no parent or master is valuable but you. However, when you begin to analyze even yourself, you will come to realize how worthless you are. The so-called intellectuals are those who cannot make head nor tail of what is valuable. If you become like them, Europe—which made you feel worthless—would become something valuable, like God."[49]

The irrationalism of the Japanese, not only in the case of this Japanist, is expressed in such words as "Things in this world do not always

---

48. Yokomitsu Riichi, *Ryoshū* [Loneliness on a Journey] (Tokyo: Kaizōsha, 1950).
49. Ibid.

stand to reason," or "Man cannot always be understood through reason." In this indiscernible portion there exists something inscrutable, which is said to be beyond analysis. The inscrutable portion is, on one hand, related to the lingering impressions and aftertaste of imperfectionism, and, on the other hand, to Japanese intuition.

In brief, Japanese irrationalism is not utter mysticism, for it recognizes rationality to a certain extent. However, it leaves a portion of ambiguous and indiscernible irrationality behind. It is, so to speak, partial or reserved irrationalism. Since such irrationalism is not consistent, inconsistency and elasticity may be said to be features of the Japanese philosophy.

For example, Ayukawa Gisuke at one point cites a concrete example from stock exchange quotations and explains his view of the changes in the economy and society not in scientific terms but by referring to fate. He says, "To make a long story short, the textile industry was unusually brisk the other day. But the next morning the market dropped sharply. No one had imagined that this would be so. Since the world is changing rapidly, it is impossible to foresee all of its changes."[50] This partial irrationalism, which takes the stand that not all of a social phenomenon is subject to rule, is at present widespread among the intellectuals of Japan.

Reason Wins

Irrationalism, as I have explained so far, is liable to be seen as a traditional psychology, something integrally part of the Japanese. But a rationalistic spirit was not entirely lacking in historic Japan.

There were a considerable number of warlords who, contending for victory in battle, put great emphasis on rationally planning maneuvers and strategy and tried to live according to a rationalistic spirit. Needless to say, this was not rationalism in the modern sense,

---

50. Ayukawa, *My Belief.*

but it did involve thinking out logical tactics, in opposition to the irrationalism that simply attributes victory or defeat to fate. This is clear in the following words of Takeda Shingen: "A defeat in war that ought not to have happened or the decline of a family that should not have occurred, all ascribe these to Heaven's decree. As far as I am concerned, I do not see it as the result of Heaven's decree but as a failure in strategy. If a prearranged strategy were carried out, there should be no defeat. Therefore, I was always solicitous that the manners of my household did not fall off and run counter to reason."[51] Shingen attributed victory or defeat in war or the decline of a family not to Heaven's decree but solely to strategy and reason. He boldly strove to do away with what he regarded as superstitions.

The battle against Ogasawara Nagatoki at Kikyōgahara is a good example of Shingen's attitude. The fight was still undecided at dusk, and the troops of both sides withdrew. The following day was an unlucky day, and Shingen said, "Nagatoki must be off guard, taking it for granted that I would not attack on an unlucky day." Following this logic, Shingen made a surprise attack the next day and won a decisive victory. It happened that when he dispatched troops to Shinshū, a dove came to perch on a tree in the garden. His vassals were delighted at the sight, saying, "A good omen for a great victory in the battle!" Hearing them, Shingen shot down the dove with a fowling piece. He did this to try to break their belief in omens, thinking that it would be embarrassing to the soldiers if a dove did not come flying the next time.[52]

In the comments in *Refutation and Correction of the Record of Kusunoki Hyōgo*, which was quoted in the section on fatalism, the fatalism expounded in the text is criticized as follows: "It is shallow to amplify the meaning of the five fates and to say, 'Never doubt them.'" The commentator obviously rejects fatalism, for he says,

---

51. Takeda Shingen, *Kōyōgunkan* [General Takeda's Book of Tactics] (1656).
    Takeda Shingen (1521–1573) was a feudal lord in Kai Province (now Yamanashi Prefecture).
52. Ibid.

"Between the heavens and the earth, men and animals, all beings, are given life according to reason. . . . The being called man is not that being if he is not fully aware of reason. . . . It is impossible to elucidate all questions by virtue of the five fates."[53]

During the Tokugawa period, in the Aizu clan, an article was added to the *Interdict for Military Men* to weaken superstition. It read: "It is prohibited to make a comment on the good or ill luck of friend or foe by talking of *yin-yang* and divination or of the fortune and misfortune of a fierce god."[54]

However, even when rationalism was adopted among the warriors as the only possible means of winning a war, it was, so to speak, a distinctive exception. Among the Japanese, rationalism appears at this time to have been part of the thinking of a small minority.

About 150 years ago Shiba Kōkan, deploring the irrationalism of the Japanese, wrote in the *Scribbles of Shunpa-rō*, "My compatriots are not keen in the investigation of natural laws. . . . People in my country are not fond of the study of all creation."[55] Even now, among professional scientists, there are very few complete rationalists and votaries of scientism. Those who live their daily life rationally are looked upon as eccentric. As I have explained before, this is an outgrowth of the irrationalism expressed in the clichés "Man is not always rational" and "Things in this world do not always stand to reason" which has permeated the minds of the Japanese.

As a result of this attitude, those who try to live rationally are apt to be misunderstood or criticized by the public. The following quotation is part of the reminiscences of Iwase Eiichirō, president of the Mitsukoshi Department Store, a man who lived a rationalized life: "In my case too there seem to be people who often criticize me, saying, 'He is a misanthrope,' or 'He is unsociable.' But I do not mind this at all. If you say that it is more human to meet a man whom I do not have to see or go to a place where I do not have

---

53. Ejima, *Refutation.*
54. *Aizu-han shisotsu kinrei* [Aizu-han Interdict for Military Men].
55. Shiba Kōkan, *Shunpa-rō hikki* [Scribbles of Shunpa-rō] (1811).

to go and make myself agreeable to everyone, I would take it as sheer nonsense. To me, if a meeting were necessary, regardless of its nature, official or private, I would be happy to go and meet others. Otherwise, needless to say, I would not spend time wastefully, for I am a very busy man."[56]

What Iwase has said sounds quite natural among Americans; however, to Japanese his words sound very inhuman and cold. In Japan it is necessary to meet people whom you do not want to see for the sake of social propriety and to spend time "wastefully." As stated in the previously cited book on the art of living, lingering impressions and waste are necessary in man's life.

Let me quote Ozaki Yukio, who declares himself more clearly a rationalist: "My philosophy is scientific rationalism. Set the basis of your thought in the same way that the basis of weights and measures is set. This serves to discriminate right from wrong in accord with science. This is the best way, for, if happiness seen by eye and happiness heard by ear are further examined scientifically and if the good that remains is set up as the basis for the construction of a society, a good society may possibly be made. Once you recognize happiness, all you have to do thereafter is to estimate things with an abacus and a rule."[57]

Since Ozaki thinks things through scientifically and sets up the actualization of a rational society as an ideal, he is able to assert positively that the Imperial Rescript on Education "is worthless. . . . I do not understand it at all. . . . It only contributed to the downfall of the country."[58] However, this view is at present still such an exception in the ruling class of Japan that it has no bearing on the majority of people.

In Japan the rationalism of sound living based on scientific knowl-

---

56. Iwase Eiichirō, *Ningen o tsukure kane o tsukure* [Develop a Fine Character and Make a Fortune] (Tokyo: Shikisha, 1952).
57. Ozaki Yukio in *Watakushi no tetsugaku* [My Philosophy], Committee for the Study of the Science of Thought, eds. (Tokyo: Chūō Kōron Sha, 1950).
58. Ibid.

edge and logic never developed. Especially after the war, pseudorationalists with an inhuman and distorted attitude began to appear. The most typical example is Yamazaki of the Hikari Club.

Life Can Be Explained by Reason

Yamazaki regarded rationalism as the main system of life. He said that if life could not be rationalized into "a life system with permanency and unity, . . . he could not possibly stand such a state any longer because he would feel physical repugnance."[59] He could not feel at rest unless he was in a fixed frame of reference. Yet he could believe neither in any existing religion nor in any ideology; therefore, he attempted to protect his fragile self within a frame of pseudorationalism of his own design. I have previously cited Yamazaki as an illustration in the section on egoism. In order to overcome his weakness of self psychologically, he thought out a "rationalism" in which the most serious problem was how to put himself and his surroundings in good order, enabling him to cope with them using definite laws and regulations.

A shortcut to the solution of this problem is to hypothesize that everything is "rationalized" beforehand. His ego is weak, unable to help him walk positively into a new situation which cannot possibly be rationalized by traditional means and cope with it. He makes his infirm ego secure by placing it in a frame of "rationalism" which he has previously constructed.

He says that he does not adopt Machiavellism that copes with problems then and there and lacks unity over time. Evidently, this is a confession that he has no confidence in setting a strong self in motion in reaction to circumstances. His rationalism, therefore, is not to cope with any situation with the strength of a firm and ob-

---

59. Yamazaki Akitsugu, *Watakushi wa giakusha* [I Pretend to Be Evil] (Tokyo: Seinen Shobō, 1950).

jective logic but to live according to his deliberately preplanned logic.

In answer to a question asked by Niwa Fumio at a discussion meeting as to whether or not he recognized something ambiguous in man's life, Yamazaki distinctly said, "I would like to come across what people call 'something ambiguous' and to be driven into a corner. . . . I myself feel there is no such thing." He then says that, much as he would like to run up against something ambiguous and "be made aware of the fallacy of my theory, . . . I have, unfortunately, not yet come up against any such thing."[60]

Yamazaki was motivated from the outset by the premise that there is nothing irrational and ambiguous in life. This does not mean that he had not come up against it, but that he had passed through this ambiguity with his eyes closed. The question of whether there is something ambiguous or not offers no problem to him, for he has previously eliminated it from his life system. According to him, either Machiavellism, resorting to trickery, or rationalism is the sole means to live surrounded by men filled with viciousness and contradictions.[61]

Inasmuch as he does not have confidence in his ability to push his way through with Machiavellism, he abides by the law as the standard of social order. However, he says that he does not admit the existence of morals and justice. Thus, despite his sticking at nothing to gain his ends, he fulfills contracts legally and rationally. What he calls "legality" means to agree with the "law" that he has thought out, and "rationality" means nothing but to apply this theory to everything.

This is not rationalism in life but rather contractualism. In short, it is subjective legitimacy in that what is contracted will be upheld completely, even if it seems irrational to common sense. He explains

---

60. Kotani Tsuyoshi, Niwa Fumio and Yamazaki Akitsugu, "Renai to jinsei to shi o kataru" ["Panel Discussion on Love, Life and Death"], *Fujinkōron* 36, no. 392 (1950).

61. Ibid.

this contractualism as follows: "I abide by the principle of international law, 'what is mutually consented to shall be binding.' I never abide by any other morality than this. . . . What is once promised should be fulfilled without fail; this is what I do, based upon my view of the world."[62]

His rationalism is based upon his view of the world; it is not rationalism based upon a scientific view of the world but is merely a distortion motivated by self-interest and selfishness. The advocacy of distortion as an excuse for self-interest is a type of pseudorationalism often found among postwar youth, an attempt to justify their behavior "rationally."

A high school girl of the postwar generation voiced her objection to being labeled a delinquent girl: "Adults readily call me a delinquent girl, seeing what I did, although I did it with good reason. . . . I really feel that I have gained more by seeing a Takarazuka show than by listening to scummy lectures at school. . . . I wouldn't have to go to Inogashira Park or the Takarazuka Theater if the Takarazuka show were held at school and if a pond were dug on campus and I could row a boat there. If that were the case I think no one would dare call me a delinquent girl."[63]

Needless to say, there must be many people, adults and children both, who have similar demands in mind. Assertions based on this kind of "reason" are a type of pseudorationalism which has become common since the war.

Let me cite a much more extreme example. A delinquent high school girl who was questioned for prostitution is said to have asserted: "This is my *arbeit*. [The term means a part-time job in Japan.] It's an individual's freedom to use his head, arms, or any part of his body for his *arbeit*." She, too, is one of pseudorationalists who "rationalize" their self-assertive behavior.

This "rationalization" is often found in postwar antisocial groups

---

62. Ibid.
63. Furuya Tsunatake, *Shōnen shōjo kara otona eno kōgi* [Protests from Boys and Girls] (Tokyo: Nishiogi Shoten, 1951).

such as *yakuza* and *panpan* (prostitutes) and seems to be an extension of pseudorationalism. They try to affirm their antisocial life openly by shaking off irrational and ambiguous sentiments. In the new type of *yakuza*, the self-punishment or self-condemnation seen in the old type of *yakuza* can not be observed; rather, they rationalize, justifying their conduct and asserting its legitimacy.

Ozu Kinosuke, the previously mentioned head of the Ozu Group, said, "I dare call myself a *yakuza* openly. . . . Are *yakuza* villains? Definitely not! The spirit of . . . what I call the way of the *yakuza* is the spirit of utter sacrifice, 'to renounce oneself and participate in justice.' . . . It is common to the Love of Christ and the Way of Bodhisattva in Buddhism."[64] The awareness of a man in the shadows is no longer present. He tacitly asserts the legitimacy of the *yakuza*, saying, "What is legitimate with a political party turns out to be illegitimate with a band of hoodlums. Is this the way of the world?"[65] This is certainly a kind of social criticism, and in that respect this way of thinking contains elements of a rationalistic view of society.

As Yamazaki rationalized his conduct according to his own law and theory, Ozu also rationalizes his course of action by using justice as a measure. He said, "Once I believe that I am just, I gain courage to persevere no matter what the odds are."[66]

There are many people, for instance, prostitutes, who have rationalized their behavior in the same way. Especially in the early stages of the American occupation, the so-called "breakwater" theory, which said that "since we sacrificially make ourselves a breakwater against the American officers and soldiers, daughters of good families are kept in safety," was a prop of their pseudorationalism.

This is certainly a type of rationalization. There is another case of rationalization which is much more honest and plain in form. There

64. Ozu Kinosuke, *Shin yakuza monogatari* [A New Yakuza Story] (Tokyo: Hayakawa Shobō, 1953).
65. Ibid.
66. Ibid.

are, for example, prostitutes who plainly write in their memoirs, "It's profitable to live pleasantly in such a life as my present one," or "Since I'm very much interested in sexual intercourse itself and it's a lucrative job, this type of life serves two ends."[67] In their pseudorationalism, the calculation of gain and loss and carnal pleasure are the criteria of judgment.

When such pseudorationalism is more consciously utilized, it develops into the cleverness found in the philosophy of life of the postwar generation. This philosophy attempts to bring a rational element into human relations, an element absent in the traditional Japanese art of living. The criterion is not ethical judgment but success; only advantages or disadvantages are taken into consideration.

In *How to Live Life Smartly Henceforth*, a new style of this rational technique of living is expounded. As a technique to make oneself look important and, contrarily, to give others a sense of superiority, it advises: "Display your true value by means of your own ability. Be a swaggerer sometimes. Plan a minor mistake once in a while to move others to laughter."[68]

An especially detailed explanation of buffoonery is given: "If you are keenly alive to your own best interests and you are trusted by others, you should deliberately make a minor mistake if only to move them to laughter. It will make you lovable and likable to your inferiors and will ease your superior's sense of vigilance against you."[69]

Contrary to the attitude taught in the traditional school of ethics that you ought wholeheartedly to do your best, this book preaches a unique imperfectionism. Generally, in your work, "if you do everything perfectly, you will at the same time create doubt"; there-

---

67. Takenaka Katsuo, *Gaishō* [Streetgirls—Actual Conditions and Their Memoirs] (Tokyo: Yūkōsha, 1949).
68. Yoshii Akira, *Korekara no jōzu na ikikata* [How to Live Smartly Henceforth] (Tokyo: Bungadō, 1952).
69. Ibid.

fore, "the best way is to do 90 percent of your assignment with your own ability and leave the rest unfinished, just for the purpose of enabling your superior to meddle and butt in."[70]

In regard to playing, the book advises, "When you relax with your fellow workers, you should always be alert not to exceed more than half of your drinking limit. If this is not enough, go to another place alone to satisfy your desires."[71]

However, the point which most obviously exhibits the "rationalism" of this philosophy is found under the heading "How to Take a Bribe." "If a patronized merchant comes with a bribe, you should refuse to accept it at first. If he forces it on you, you should take it gladly. But . . . give no word of promise. . . ." If the bribe is money, entertain him with your money or buy him something in return; if it is a gift, send him a gift of equal value. It is his goodwill that makes him give you a bribe; therefore, the book advises that if you refuse the bribe flatly, you will "incur his ill feeling and it might turn out to be the cause of a pretty mess."[72]

In Japan people in all positions, from government officials to the bottom of the social ladder, take bribes, but this is probably the first book which instructs the reader how to take a bribe creditably. This is the epitome of postwar pseudorationalism. The author next describes his faith without hesitation: "The way to live skillfully depends on one's know-how, how one can make the means and actual condition of life, which can never be a clean thing, look like a clean thing."[73] Such a statement, which exhibits postwar rationalism so honestly, is indeed unusual.

The fact that such an attitude has spread not only to adults but also to children is clear in the following frank words: "But if the school allowed us to play hooky, I guess no pupil would come to

---

70. Ibid.
71. Ibid.
72. Ibid.
73. Ibid.

school. Isn't it to our mutual benefit that we pupils play smartly and well?"[74]

Needless to say, smartness is not an exclusive product of the post-war period. As I have previously mentioned, it existed in the army. In fact, in the books which expound attentiveness for warriors, many examples can be found if one reads carefully. In the *Hagakure* many techniques useful for warriors in living their lives are recorded. For example, under the heading "Attitude in Times of Dispute" the following advice is given: "Be quite agreeable. Let your opponent state his mind. When he says too much, taking a victory for granted, you should find his sore spot, change your attitude, and argue against him as much as you want." It also advises that in case of a dispute such as litigation or controversy, it is best to make your attitude undecided, leaving a margin for another day saying, "I will ponder it and answer you later," or "I will muse over it further," and ask various other persons for advice. Moreover, a man who looks clever is "not conspicuous, even if he does fine work. . . . Yet if he works like others, he is thought to be under par." On the contrary, "a man who looks gentle will be praised by all when he acts slightly conspicuous."[75] Each of these examples is a technique for living and differs greatly from the customary solemn posture based on the five virtues of benevolence, righteousness, politeness, intelligence, and faithfulness.

Nevertheless, since in Japan the attitude manifested in the saying "Sincerity moves Heaven" originating in irrationalism and spiritualism has long been taken as a formula for the art of living, the sensible posture propounded above seems, inversely, to be unwarriorlike. As a result, the part of the *Hagakure* which gives tenets of living appears to be foreign to the overall irrational tone.

---

74. Furuya, *Protests*.
75. Yamamoto, *Shade of Leaves*.

5. Spiritualism and Physicality

Firm Determination Pierces Even a Rock

A phase of the Japanese psychology connected with irrationalism is spiritualism, which still wields strong influence. "Spiritualism" here refers to both the idea that the spirit surpasses the body or matter in some way, and to the actions resulting from that idea. It assumes a number of forms among the Japanese.

First, it is a conviction that man can do the unexpected and superhuman when his "spiritual force" works upon a condition that seems to be beyond human wisdom and strength. In a second form, it is the idea that a spirit can function to change material conditions. Another manifestation is the view that every substance has a spirit, that is, hylozoism, the theory of oneness of matter and spirit.

In the first aspect of spirituality, what is considered from the standpoint of irrationalism to be beyond man's power owing to the control of Heaven's decree and fate is thought to be at the disposal of the spirit or spiritual force.

Such proverbs as "Nothing is impossible to a determined mind," "Sincerity moves Heaven," "Firm determination pierces even a rock," and "Even an ant's wish reaches Heaven," are expressions of this type of spiritualism. Moving Heaven, that is, Heaven's decree or fate, by the spirit or by a sincere wish not only reveals the effect of enthusiasm and exertion but also shows that what is beyond rational wisdom or resource can be fulfilled by irrational and mysterious spiritual strength.

Spiritualism, the belief that the spirit displays superhuman power under conditions actually beyond human wisdom or judged to be beyond human wisdom was quite dominant among Japanese military men. "The situation was already beyond the control of human wisdom. This being so, there could be no other means to achieve a miracle except the pure and innocent spirit of these youth and their fresh vigor to retain their spiritual purity,"[1] wrote the authors of *The Kamikaze Suicide Units.*

Although they said, "beyond human wisdom," in actuality they wished for a miracle in order to avert the imminent defeat of the Japanese forces obvious to human wisdom. If they believed that a miracle could have been achieved through the spirit and vigor of the youth, they should be called the worst representatives of Japanese spiritualism.

Spiritualism, however, was not limited to military men who held positions of command. Yoshida Mitsuru, second sub-lieutenant and sub-radar officer and author of the *Battleship Yamato*, describes his spiritualistic attitude just before the final battle. "Meanwhile, during a few days' rest, I will gain the mental strength to turn the tide of the war and will cultivate my fighting spirit for sure death in a state of perfect selflessness."[2]

In fact, in the Japanese army, to have faith in sure death or sure victory superseded scientific strategy. The worse the situation became, the more rational methods were rejected; the more a miracle based on spiritualism was expected, the worse the situation became: obviously, a vicious circle. An army officer talks of his experiences with this attitude: "Although this is the peak of spiritualism, we are ordered to cook up an ingenious plan or some secret art or trick practiced by someone like Chu-ko K'ung-ming. What is that but conjuring or magic? There are no books to teach us. The order is simply 'Do it.'"[3] When defeat drew near, spiritualism rather than

---

1. Inokuchi Rikihei and Nakajima Tadashi, *Kamikaze tokubetsu kōgekitai* [The *Kamikaze* Suicide Units] (Tokyo: Nihon Shuppan Kyōdō Kabushiki Gaisha, 1951).

2. Yoshida Mitsuru, *Senkan Yamato no saigo* [The Final Day of the Battleship *Yamato*] (Tokyo: Sōgensha, 1952).

3. Iizuka Kōji, *Nihon no guntai* [The Japanese Military] (Tokyo: Tokyo Daigaku Shuppanbu, 1950).

scientism, faith rather than technique, was stressed. This tendency was revealed in the spirit of the suicide units.

In answer to a question asked by the American Board of Inquiry on Bombing meeting after the war, Lieutenant Colonel Inokuchi of the *kamikaze* suicide units said, "Originally, the *kamikaze* suicide units possessed a spiritual character. As far as technical skill was concerned, a member could achieve the aims if he had the skill of an ordinary pilot."[4] As is obvious from this reply, military education based on spiritualism placed mental cultivation above scientific and technical training, so that even in the suicide units, as far as technical skill was concerned, ordinary skill was sufficient.

In the conditioning of military men, "Japanism" or the military spirit was said to oppose theory. Moreover, military education was itself spiritualistic. For example, the Imperial Mandate was preached without any interpretation of its phraseology so that the men would "feel" its value. " 'Read the words and phrases of the Imperial Mandate, whether you understand them or not. While reading them, you will appreciate their savor and the Imperial Mandate will truly turn into your blood and flesh.' . . . 'Read them every day.'— that is what we were told. After one or two years, strangely enough we came to feel that the Imperial Mandate was somehow valuable."[5]

What is not conceivable is valuable, this is the doctrine of spiritualism. The inconceivable is said to be "conceived" not by the intellect but by the spirit.

Everything Depends on Your Attitude

Spiritualism also is the belief that the spirit can, in actuality, alter material conditions. When this faith is applied to life, it becomes a view of spiritual happiness which holds that material privation can

---

4. Inokuchi and Nakajima, *Suicide Units.*
5. Iizuka, *Japanese Military.*

be relieved by something spiritual, that happiness depends largely upon one's attitude. This view of spiritual happiness is equivalent to the attitude that suffering and pleasure all depend upon one's attitude, which has traditionally been recommended as the easiest access to happiness.

The joyous life of Tenrikyō previously mentioned is a life lived with a mind of clear sky no matter how hard things may be. This is accomplished by bravely living life with a switchover of mind. "Don't look for the whereabouts of hell or paradise. It is latent in each individual's mind."[6]

A book on self-cultivation reads: "If happiness is gained in the spiritual world, we are happy, even though we are more or less unhappy in this world." It also says that "a favorable condition or an unfavorable condition can never be a fact of life but depends upon one's attitude."[7]

In the postwar view of spiritual happiness, how to attain a sense of happiness is not mentioned very often. The following mention is a rare one. "Somewhere a man would discover the feeling of 'I'm happy' even if he were poor, sick, oppressed, and unhappy."[8]

In contrast to this attitude, when Japanism was the core of spiritualism, the military spirit, as the essence of Japanism, was thought to control material conditions. During the war, the following instruction concerning the problem of food for the prisoners of war was given by the head of a concentration camp:

> Under the circumstances, when food is in short supply throughout land, we cannot afford to give enough food to the prisoners. . . . Traditionally, in our country, there has been Japanism. The crystallization of Japanism is the military spirit. If you are full

6. Ikoma Fujio, *Tenrikyo yōgi* [The Essentials of *Tenrikyō*] (Tanbaichi-cho, Nara Ken: Tenrikyo Jihōsha, 1948).

7. Tamura Reishō, *Omakase to jinsei* [Passivity and Life] (Tokyo: Tenshindō-honbu, 1942).

8. Nihei Kazutsugu, *Ikinuku seikatsu* [A Life That Has to Be Lived Through] (Tokyo: Kōfūkan, 1951).

of the military spirit and come in contact with the prisoners resolutely, it will brace up their state of mind. Despite being spoiled by material civilization, they will eventually come to perceive of spirit as above the material, bear privations, overcome such an effeminate sickness as malnutrition, and extensively cooperate in an increase of production.[9]

This instruction reveals most plainly an important phase of Japanese spiritualism, the disregard for material and life.

In the Japanese army, this spiritualism was incessantly emphasized as something more important than material conditions in battle. "What decides the fate of a war depends upon the degree of the mental blow rather than upon material damage." A staff officer of the suicide units said, "When the crisis of the country has come . . . viewed from the angle of the wide difference in war potential between us and the enemy, the time to offer ourselves for the sake of His Majesty [this includes the concept of fatherland] has indeed come." Living up to this spiritualism, he organized suicide units, knowing that "the people of European countries would criticize it as an attempt made out of despair and would look upon it as foul play." The Japanese traditionally "lay their spiritual ground of life and death on absolute submission to a greater authority and disregard for their lives."[10] In these cases, the lives of those who were participating in the war and the material conditions of the military are totally ignored and are lightly dismissed as "the wide difference in war potential between us and the enemy."

In the most extreme cases, spiritualism during the war took the form of a "spiritual charge." It was indeed the peak of spiritualism to believe that the departed souls of a totally annihilated unit could rout the enemy; that is to say, that despite the loss of life, victory could be won. For example, "When a unit made a dash at an upland

9. Iizuka Kōji, *Arekara shichinen* [Seven Years Have Passed] (Tokyo: Kōbunsha, 1953).

10. Inokuchi and Nakajima, *Suicide Units*.

at Nomonhan, the unit was wiped out. However, the enemy must have felt uneasy, for they gave up the position and retreated. For that reason, this staff officer said, 'How do you men look at this incident? The departed souls were still making a charge. Is it not a fact that the enemy retreated?' "[11]

There were many military men who were very religious and believed, even in the case of total annihilation, "No, we are not defeated! Rather, we die to be reborn in the Takamagahara [Plain of High Heaven]. . . . Complete annihilation on Attu Island . . . the dead were united into something sublime." In fact, when defeat drew near, the shocking idea of complete annihilation as a type of spiritualism was discussed among the leaders of the army who took a crushing defeat of all the armies and the sacrifice of a whole people for granted for the defense of Japan proper. "Even if we were to be wiped out on each battlefield, a 'spiritual charge' would be further carried out on a nationwide scale."[12] In this logic of the "spiritual charge," even bamboo spear resistance was not considered reckless.

When the end of the war was near, a "Decree for Defense against Disembarkation" was distributed among officers on the pretext of offering a countermeasure to the enemy landing on Japanese shores. "Under the painful conditions of the wide difference in war potential between us and the enemy, . . . for the purpose of winning a victory" it is necessary for "soldiers to have great spiritual strength and a firm unity. . . . Soldiers, you must firmly hold to your faith in certain victory, even if you are the last to survive, and attend to your duty."[13] No concrete strategies were ever thought out. Thus, Japanese spiritualism came to be a synonym for defeatism both on the battlefield and in life.

---

11. Iizuka, *Japanese Military*.
12. Ibid.
13. Ibid.

You Will Be Punished if You Step on a Book

The third category of spiritualism is hylozoism, which sees spirit in all matter. It is further divided into two types: hylozoism in a wide sense, which holds that all matter possesses a spirit or mind; and hylozoism in a narrow sense, in which only certain matter is felt to possess spirit.

I will not deal with hylozoism in the wide sense, pantheism, here because Japanese hylozoism is uniquely narrow. All matter is roughly divided into two, matter possessed of a spirit and matter not possessed of a spirit. For instance, a book, regarded as a product of mental work, is even now perceived by many Japanese people as matter pregnant with spirit and not matter made simply of paper and print. If this perception is accepted, a book should not be treated as a mere object. The Japanese have been taught that it is most improper to nap with one's head pillowed on a book or to use books as a stool. Americans unconcernedly sit on books in place of a stool and make good use of them for every possible purpose besides reading as long as the books are not marred. To Japanese students and teachers, this is desecration.

In Japan it is said that "a fool is he who lends or returns books." The lending or borrowing of a book differs from lending or borrowing other articles. The lender is hesitant in pressing the borrower to return the book, while the borrower is not very careful about returning it. It seems that the spiritual value lingering in a book makes the parties feel the loan is something special. This is after all a revelation of spiritualism: a book is a product of mental work, which is superior to physical work, and from the standpoint of spiritualism it is respected as spiritual matter.

A book is valued as a spiritual product, and the place of spiritual work, a desk, is treated in the same manner. Sitting on a desk and putting one's feet on it are often seen among Americans; to the Japanese this seems not only ill-mannered but sacrilegious.

The hylozoism attributed to certain matter by the Japanese people seems to be gradually fading. However, when Japanism based upon emperor worship was stressed, hylozoism was clamorously expounded in the name of the Emperor. Needless to say, extreme examples of it were found everywhere in the army.

" 'Each rifle bears the Imperial insignia. A rifle corroded with rust means corruption of its owner's military spirit.' In that way, a rifle was valued as a symbol of the military spirit.... Therefore, the harshness of a scolding depended on what part was damaged."[14] An ex-officer recalled that to handle a rifle roughly was a desecration of the military spirit and was considered an act of irreverence toward the Emperor. Moreover, since a rifle was treated as a human being possessed of a spirit, in case a rifle was damaged the degree of the offense would depend on which part was damaged.

A Sense of Collapse, written by Noma Hiroshi, tells of a scene of punishment imposed upon a second-class private who had damaged a rifle. " 'Mr. 38 M Rifle, I, Second-Class Private Oikawa Ryūichi, am a donkey, a dunce, and a fool. I have injured your precious head by mistake. I will never make such a mistake as this again, so please forgive me.' . . . This Oikawa Ryūichi was beaten with a wooden chair, dragged down to the cold dirt floor, and forced to sit on it because he broke the spring of Rifle No. 10296 while repairing it."[15] Second-Class Private Oikawa, who was taught the hylozoic nature of a rifle through corporal punishment, was a victim of barbarous hylozoism perpetrated in the name of the Emperor.

The spiritualism of the army developed into a faith in the hylozoic nature or physical effect of language. For instance, in the army, the word "retreat" could be used only in a situation where the recovery of superiority of the spirit was certain despite damage to life and materials. If this were not the case, the word "shift" would be used.

---

14. Ibid.

15. Noma Hiroshi, "Hōkai kankaku" ["A Sense of Collapse"], *Sekai Hyōron* 1–3 (1943).

This clearly reveals the physical deterioration of fighting efficiency caused by the psychological effect of a word.

It is an old story now, but in the Russo-Japanese War, a bread called *jūshō-pan* was purposely pronounced *omoyaki-pan* because the word *jūshō* also means "serious injury." There are many similar examples.

The hylozoic nature, the magic, of language is of course still the reason for coining many slang words, not only limited to the army but prevalent in the gay quarters, where superstitions prevail, and among long-established merchants. Since the word *nashi* (pear) is homonymous with *nashi* (nothing), it is often pronounced *arinomi*; the word *cha* (tea) is part of *ocha o hiku* (have no engagement), so it is sometimes pronounced *debana*; and *suru* (grind and rub) also means "loss," so *ataru* is often substituted for it: the word *suribachi* (earthenware mortar) is replaced by *ataribachi*, *surikogi* (wooden pestle) by *ataribō*, and *suzuribako* (inkstone case) by *ataribako*. In a *rakugo* comic story, a geisha girl, in answer to the question of a rickshaw man, says that her destination is "Ode no mizu bashi no Ataridai" instead of "Ocha no mizu bashi no Surugadai" (Surugadai of the Ochanomizu Bridge).

At the beginning of the Shōwa period, around 1926, the Japanese government was accused of being communistic for using the term *keikaku keizai* (planned economy). The wording was changed to *keizai keikaku* (economy plan), another example of the Japanese awareness of words.

In the different styles of expression in the Japanese language, the Imperial language, which was especially difficult in order to enhance the authority of the Emperor, made the greatest use of the spiritualism of words. The words that were used were written illegibly in characters which the masses could neither read nor understand if they heard them pronounced. The incomprehensibility and difficulty were thought suitable to show the inaccessible might of the Imperial Household. A society where the language itself, even in contemporary times, could become one of the influential powers politically and materially is rare among so-called civilized countries.

Loyalty and Filial Piety Are Good for the Health

In Japan, opposition to irrationalism, instead of developing properly into scientific rationalism, strayed into pseudorationalism and smartness. Similarly, instead of the spread of scientific materialism in opposition to spiritualism as a philosophy of life, excess physicality has become conspicuous in postwar society.

Physicality has two meanings. First, it is the idea that the physical conditions of man's life are as important as the spirit's function, which is a negative opposition to spiritualism's overemphasis on the spirit. Secondly, it is the recognition of the superiority, in some senses, of the body over spirit, a positive physicality.

Negative physicality is, in actuality, common sense. The proverbs "A soldier cannot march on an empty stomach," "Dumplings rather than blossoms," "While there is life, there is hope," and "Who can enjoy flower-viewing after he's dead?" illustrate this. Yet in Japan, these matter-of-fact proverbs have been traditionally regarded as indecent. This attitude is undoubtedly good evidence that spiritualism is deep-rooted.

Many Japanese writers and scholars claim that they have to sit upright at a desk, otherwise they are unable to write. This is a vestige of spiritualism: an uncomfortable physical position is necessary to uplift the spirit. From the point of view of physicality as common sense, in order to concentrate fully, one's physical position should be good. In other words, it would be better to do the work not by acting properly but by relaxing and making oneself as comfortable as possible. Therefore, it would be helpful to mental work if one's constitution were built up by nourishing food and outdoor exercise rather than by doing penance and performing purification.

This physicality tends to be despised and rejected from the standpoint of spiritualism as idle, slovenly, piggishly gorging, and mean deportment. In Japanese school education, especially in the past in public schools, this type of spiritualism was employed. As a result, those who have received an old-fashioned education are apt to see free and unrestricted teaching methods as slovenly. The growth of a liberal spirit is hardly to be expected if one's body is unnecessarily subjected to pressure. One of the biggest mistakes that Japan's education system ever made was the adoption of this distorted spiritualism contrary to sound physicality.

There are, of course, some old-fashioned self-cultivation books which are quite attentive to conditions of the body. *Instructions for the Preservation of Health* written by Kaibara Ekiken is a good example. He describes *yōjō no jutsu* (the art of preserving health) together with *shinjutsu* (the art of the mind) as spiritual training. *Yōjō no jutsu* is, however, a part of spiritualism, for it is based on the word *osoruru* (fear) and is grounded on the principle, "Be afraid of the Way of Heaven, be prudent, and obey. Be afraid of avarice, be prudent, and endure"[16] I would not say that this is stoicism, but it does call for a moderate control of passion and is an order to work for sanitation and preservation of health as a means of self-cultivation rather than to promote one's health as an end in itself.

Not only in the case of Ekiken but also in self-cultivation books of the Tokugawa period, there are many expressions of the view that the elevation of the mind is good for the health. This view might be called "spiritual physicality."

To cite an instance, the *Sequel to Kyuo's Moral Discourses*, a *shingaku* book, describes this view in the following way: "All who are loyal and dutiful do not suffer ill-health from cold and heat. It is because their minds are always on the alert and they have no unguarded moments. A cold is unable to watch for an unguarded moment. . . .

---

16. Kaibara Ekiken, *Yōjōkun* [Instructions for the Preservation of Health] (1713).

Loyalty and filial piety are not only virtues but are also, first, ingenious arts for preservation of the body and for longevity."[17]

Apart from books on the way of the warrior or other books on self-cultivation, the encouragement of loyalty and filial piety as not only virtuous but ingenious arts for good health is part of the morality of the townsmen, who valued material gain highly. The view is quite interesting as an illustration of a shift from Confucianist spiritualism to physicality.

In the same book, *shingaku* is defined as "a good message with which to protect oneself throughout one's life." Moreover, it describes the "art of making a comfortable living from the cradle to the grave . . . without paying for a carriage," in contrast to the comfort of travel in a palanquin. "Would you listen carefully, at least resisting your sleepy spell?"[18] Sleepy you may be, but listen to what I tell you because you can live in comfort for life. In this respect it considers the body, a townsmanlike attitude foreign to the practice of spiritualism.

The Body Is an Asset

The second type, a positive physicality, is a tendency to believe that the body is superior to spirit. It is further divided into emphasis on one's physical condition and emphasis on sexual desire and sensual pleasures.

Since spiritualism has deeply permeated the daily life of the Japanese people, the social psychology of the Americans with its emphasis on physical attributes seems strange to the Japanese. In America, when a man is evaluated or introduced, his physical attributes are also mentioned. Therefore, in an American character sketch, descriptions of height, weight, eye color, and hair color are often included.

---

17. Kyūō, *Zoku Kyūō dōwa* [Sequel to Kyūō's Moral Discourses] (1835).
18. Ibid.

In some cases, the good or bad quality of a man's tone of voice is described.

This is a unique aspect of American social psychology not found even in Europe. This keen concern for the body can be called a sort of physicality. The fact that the physical stamina to fight against the natural conditions in America was indispensable to frontier life has most likely remained as a traditional preoccupation in present-day life. At the same time, Americans' liking for figures and computation seems to be a factor involved. Knowledge pertaining to physical attributes has been so widely popularized that in one American I.Q. test there are questions such as "What is the average height of American women?" Because, generally speaking, American people, regardless of sex, take an interest in others countenances, American publications often show the author's portrait.

In Japan since the war this type of physicality has gradually been growing as a result of American influence. Postwar books, for instance, tend to include the author's picture. In the psychological tradition of Japanese spiritualism, a book is a product of an author's mental work; his appearance has nothing to do with his work. Prewar readers approached the author of a book spiritually, and his physical attributes drew no attention. Now, physicality is revealed in the fact that the portraits of writers and celebrities are shown in the frontispieces of literary or general magazines. This is an indication that readers are no longer satisfied with making the acquaintance of writers only through their works but demand some knowledge of their physical characteristics.

Men's summer short-sleeved shirts and shorts also seem to be evidence of the influence of physicality in terms of dispensing with the formalities of spiritualism and adopting physically comfortable conditions in daily living, though economical reasons should not be overlooked.

Physicality that acknowledges the body as surpassing the spirit has deeply influenced the psychology of the present-day Japanese as an important social phenomenon. Physicality in this respect stems from the conviction, acquired through the war and postwar experiences, that the body and strength are the sole capital. It also stems from the reflection that the Japanese forces, relying upon spiritual strength, were defeated by the American forces blessed with material resources and nourishment.

When a man relies solely on his body, his physical strength rather than his mental capacity naturally figures as a major portion of his entire vitality. In postwar literary works, a man possessing vital energy is often depicted as a champion of physicality. For instance, a dischargee recalls: "I had such vigor that I would do anything for a living. Anyway, there would be no new start if I did not hurl myself at the chaotic conditions with my very body."[19]

To the soldiers on a battlefield, only physical exercises gave evidence of their substance; mental functions provided no help for survival, so men stopped depending on them. Therefore, "just to make sure of my existence, I ate, drank, slept, fought against the enemy, chased after women. . . . And I was enraptured by being alive."[20]

As for the intellectuals in the cities who were exposed to the danger of air raids, their mental functions tended to keep them from surviving: "Sometimes he felt that it would be best to be done with it all and to be called into the army. If only he could escape from the anguish of thinking, even bullets and starvation might seem a blessing."[21]

When the war ended, the physicality observed during the war shifted to a social psychology in which the body was highly valued as providing the vitality needed to live through the chaos after the defeat.

Since prostitutes are very conscious of men's physical qualities,

---

19. Tamura Taijirō, *Kiri* [Fog] (Tokyo: Asashi Shoin, 1948).
20. Ibid.
21. Sakaguchi Ango, "Hakuchi" ["The Idiot"], George Saito, trans., in *Modern Japanese Stories, An Anthology*, Ivan I. Morris, ed. (Tokyo: Charles E. Tuttle Co., 1961), p. 173.

they respect muscular men as possessors of vitality. "Among her fellow prostitutes, a man like Ibuki Shintarō, who possessed more than enough fighting power for survival, was considered somehow a reliable man. All held him in awe."[22] Such a man tries to live vigorously, taking what he wants by force, as his physical strength and vitality spurt out. "He made his confidence in his tough body almost a faith. He could be distinctly aware of the strength latent in his body. He had no feeling of despair. He was living in accord with the respiration and impulse of life, generated incessantly from his innermost self. Rare, indeed, is one so bright and optimistic.[23]"

After the war, the majority of the Japanese people, who had neither physical strength nor wealth, authority, or anything else implied by the word "power," were envious but also respectful of the possessors of what they were lacking. This might be called a "faith in power." To have faith in power is to praise the possessors of power or the state of being filled with power, regardless of moral and social values. Therefore, especially now, those who feel lethargic take impudence and "nerve" as revelations of power and put a high value on them instead of regarding them with antipathy and hatred.

Faith in power and praise of the powerful, however, are not necessarily social phenomena unique to postwar times. When the masses for some reason are caught up in lethargy, there arises a longing for powerful men to fill the vacuum.

In 1936, in the postscript to *Strange Tale from East of the River,* Nagai Kafū spoke of faith in power as it emerged in the social psychology of that time through Kojiro Sōyō, an old man:

The prevalence of sports, dance, travel, mountain climbing, horse racing, and other gambling, all is a phenomenon developed out of desire. . . . Each man hopes to show that he is superior to others and to believe in his being so. That's the feeling. That's the desire

---

22. Tamura Taijiro, "Nikutai no mon" ["The Gate of the Flesh"], *Gunzō* 2, no. 3 (1947).

23. Ibid.

to have superiority over others. . . . Of the happenings in this world, . . . if you take everything as a phenomenon of energy expansion, you do not necessarily have to frown upon assassination, adultery, and whatever else may take place. . . . This is the difference between modern people, who grew to manhood during the Taishō period, and us.[24]

Since the energy in the phenomenon of energy expansion is thrown into sports, dance, travel, mountain climbing, and gambling, there are more leisure activities. The prevalence of dance and gambling results from the energies of the masses which could not find any serious vent in politics, culture, and learning. The faith in power found satisfaction nowhere but in dance and gambling.

In the same work, Kafū delineates a scene at a *sushi* stand in a back street which resembles many postwar scenes: "How extremely the moderns . . . try to compete for supremacy. . . . Once they find out that the stand is crowded, their eyes immediately become piercing, and they push through the crowd as soon as they see a vacant seat. . . . They do not hesitate to thrust women and children off the platform to secure a vacant seat in a train." However, Kafū attributes this sense of superiority to a hard world different from the easy old days. He sees the difference between the Meiji people who attended school on foot and the present-day people who have jumped into a crowded streetcar ever since they were schoolchildren as the source of this new attitude.[25]

The prevalence of dancing and gambling is not explained only by the hustle and bustle and struggle for existence. People, after all, build up competitive and offensive feelings as a result of various pent-up grievances and dissatisfactions with mundane matters. This is true today. People scramble for a ride in a bus or streetcar and waste more time, despite the fact that they could easily

24. Nagai Kafū, *Bokutō kidan* [A Strange Tale from East of the River] (Tokyo: Asahi Shimbun Sha, 1937).
25. Ibid.

get a ride if they would wait a minute longer. Since people today are always irritated by these minor hostilities, unnecessary hustling, jostling, and scrambling take their place as one of the minor vents for these feelings.

Competition for supremacy also takes place because people do, on the other hand, feel inferior and lethargic. In order to forget one's inferiority and lethargy and to feel superior to others for a moment, it seems good to push others aside, hit the jackpot, win a game of chance. Herein lies one of the psychological sources of faith in power.

Kafū made an observation regarding this faith in power in *A Tale Told by a Housemaid*: "Even in daily conversation, I hear numerous newly coined words that I never heard when the world was tranquil. Among them, the phrases most frequently used are 'live strongly' and 'be strong.' However, these words seem to be used with the opposite meaning if circumstances require it." He then cites a popular song "learned by chance at a bar in a back street: '. . . whatever will be, will be. Even the sadly sinking evening sun will come up in the morning. Please be strong. Darling, please be strong.'" He concludes the story with a description of Emiko, a maid: "She is what is called in this world one of the strong. . . . She seems to be strong, she who cries herself to sleep, thinking that even the sadly sinking evening sun will come up brightly after the night passes."[26] Kafū also uses words such as "admiration of the strong," which is said to be psychologically grounded in the lethargy of the weak.

Since the war, the vitality of the prostitute, delinquent youngster, black-market profiteer, and gangster has been valued from the point of view of faith in power; many people secretly envy and admire this type of conduct rather than resenting it. Before judging the propriety of their so-called antisocial conduct, people become fascinated and impressed by their fearlessness and strength.

---

26. Nagai Kafū, *Jochū no hanashi* [A Tale Told by a Housemaid] (Tokyo: Chūō Kōron Sha, 1938).

A man who wants to believe that he himself has such power to any degree tends to display it in some form. Yamazaki of the Hikari Club said, "I just wanted to try to the limit of my ability. . . . I wished to appreciate the beauty of my life's complete combustion by betting my fifty-year-long life in this big month-long gamble, . . . to experience the lively thrill of moneymaking even at the risk of my life."[27]

As I have mentioned before, Yamazaki, who wished to try his ability, believed in power. However, he possessed a feeble self, although he wished all the more to believe that he was strong. Faith in power is a faith for the weak.

When You Talk about Love, You Mean Physical Desire

The sensual literature of Tamura Taijirō looks at faith in power as vitality in the world of prostitutes and gangs. According to him, in man's life "only the flesh is reality." Since man "is able to be aware of his existence through his flesh, . . . there is no such act as thought apart from flesh."[28] Physicality of this sort naturally comes to be connected with sex as a physical demand and becomes a sexual physicality.

Sexual physicality means, first, the emancipation of love and sex, both of which were unreasonably suppressed in Japan's society up until the defeat. In this respect, this type of physicality is a liberation from feudalistic sexual morality and certainly comprises wholesome elements. It is not a fair view simply to object to sexualism, viewing it as sexual decadence.

The emancipation of sex, of course, has gone on to excessive

27. Yamazaki Akitsugu, *Watakushi wa giakusha* [I Pretend to Be Evil] (Tokyo: Seinen Shobō, 1950).

28. Tamura Taijirō, "Nikutai ga ningen de aru" ["The Flesh Is the Human Being"], *Gunzō* 2, no. 5 (1947).

decadence with the emergence of the striptease and the sale of prohibited books, cheap magazines, and erotic evening papers. However, as Sakaguchi Ango said, "Those who deplore such phenomena, saying, 'Public morals are corrupted,' know nothing of the world and talk in their sleep." It might be said that "what has been hidden in back of an orderly society is simply coming to the surface after the defeat."[29]

Whether sexual decadence is on the surface or under the surface makes a great difference, something like the difference between pus which remains in a sore or oozes out. Sexual decadence is, of course, an embarrassing problem; however, it is, to a certain extent, unavoidable in the process of its own exhaustion.

Sexual liberation, especially the dissemination of sexual knowledge, would be good sex education even for adults, if properly directed. A striptease satisfies one's curiosity about what has been hidden, the physical beauty of the female form. The curiosity of the masses is not only directed toward sex but toward the satisfaction of their wants, so they try to discover the facts kept from them until the defeat. Their curiosity is a revelation of their attachment to fact.

Sexual liberation has not been achieved only for the sake of sensuality. Spectators at a striptease these days heckle and laugh at the performance; however, when stripping was new in Japan, people would watch the show with a solemn look, evidence of a spirit of inquiry into mysterious facts. They were utterly different from spectators of a striptease abroad. Lately, the adults of Japan have graduated from the sexual education level and now enjoy watching in a carefree manner.

Risqué books and erotic magazines seem to have been harmful, on the one hand; however, the emergence of such publications was, to some extent, inevitable in order for adults to move beyond the first degree of eroticism and move toward healthy sexual emancipation. Observing the trials connected with *Lady Chatterley's Lover* and

29. Sakaguchi Ango, *Zoku daraku ron* [The Sequel to "On Corruption"] (Tokyo: Ginza Shuppansha, 1947).

listening to the opinions of its readers, it may be said that common knowledge on sex is broader than during prewar times and is progressing in the right direction.

Sexualism is also revealed in connection with the distrust of postwar youth of humanity in general. When a man is unable to trust others, only he himself seems trustworthy. The only proof that reaffirms his existence is his physical body. To a young physician depicted in *Positive Proof* by Kotani Tsuyoshi, his six years of debauched living was upheld as a fight based on self, and "the sole 'positive proof' of a victory of the self was to affirm the existence of his body."[30] Self is not upheld by spirit but its assertion is secured by the reaffirmation of the body. A phrase common in postwar sensual literature is "restoration of the spirit using the body."

Tanaka Hidemitsu in his work *Pain in Love and Hatred* describes his association with a prostitute in the following way: "While loving her smooth flesh, I have come to realize that our love, though at the outset we were only after sensual gratification, is now attended by a sense of satisfaction originating from passionate spiritual love."[31]

Tanaka in his novel *Apart from the Soul* described his relationship with this woman. Although he was a spiritualist—he did not know what sexual love was until he reached the age of thirty-six, and he tried to avoid having carnal desire for women to whom he felt attached—he came to think that "love between man and woman is to bare to each other all their sense of shame, wherein lies relief in life." He was overwhelmed by the unrestrained passion of the woman.[32]

Generally, and not only in the case of Tanaka, spiritualism forms an essential part of the Japanese view of love. The traditional saying, "a courtesan sells her flesh but not her mind," reflects the separation

---

30. Kotani Tsuyoshi, *Kakushō* [Positive Proof] (Tokyo: Kaizōsha, 1949).
31. Tanaka Hidemitsu, *Ai to nikushimi no kizuni* [Pain in Love and Hatred] (Tokyo: Getsuyō Shobō, 1949).
32. Tanaka Hidemitsu, *Rikon* [Apart from the Soul], *Shin Shosetsu* 4, no. 8 (1949).

of the physical act of sex and the spiritual act of love in the Japanese mind. The idea persists that spiritual or Platonic love without intimate relations is possible and much nobler than sexual love that is physically fulfilled.

Thus there arises the idea that even if one has experienced sexual relations, one can retain spiritual purity. "A woman makes much of her virginity; she loses all her purity, once she is deflowered. That's how she degrades herself into a woman of the streets. You know, purity is not so ephemeral. It is inherent in the spirit. I believe all housewives in Japan, regardless of the fact that they have lost their virginity and changed husbands five or ten times, ought to have purity of spirit."[33]

Needless to say, purity or impurity is not judged only by a person's physical condition; it is questionable whether or not one can retain purity regardless of having physical contact. On the other hand, in Japanese public offices the word "purity" is used in terms of spiritualism, and the words "education for purity" are substituted for the term "sex education." The officials' basic idea seems to be to equate physical relationships with impurity.

Spiritualism in sex is revealed in the attitude that finds prostitution permissible as a business deal but sensual pleasure a vice among prostitutes. "It is not a vice to sell their flesh for those prostitutes who do not know the pleasures of the organic functions. It is merely a deal. Vice lies in a prostitute indulging in sensual pleasures without being paid."[34]

The idea that an intimate relationship with a prostitute is forgivable but sex beyond a mere business deal is immoral was prevalent in the past. For instance, a wife delineated in *Chattering Bathers in a Public Bathhouse* by Shikitei Sanba gives her opinion about men's extramarital affairs: "Whoring is forgivable, for there is a limit to it. What are evil and embarrassing are the relations with *jimono* [non-

---

33. Sakaguchi Ango, *Ao-oni no fundoshi o arau onna* [A Woman Who Washes the Loincloth of a Green Ogre] (Tokyo: Yamane Shoten, 1947).

34. Tamura, *Gate of the Flesh.*

professionals]. . . . If you are a man, you'd better get a woman you pay."[35] It is neither wanton nor immoral to buy the services provided by so-called professional women. This old-fashioned attitude seems to be warrantable at the present time among the mesdames of high society, who feel that it is permissible for celebrated men who deplore the deterioration of morality to go on geisha sprees or keep mistresses. This, too, is a misinterpretation stemming from spiritualism in sex.

To deny spiritual love and to see love as having two sides, spiritual and physical, is the denial of spiritualism in love and is a physical view of love. This may seem to be carnalism or lewdness, from the spiritualist point of view; however, the idea that love is motivated by desire is distinctly manifested, for example, in the thought of Motoori Norinaga. He discusses love poems in his *Whispered Words of the Past*, written in 1736, saying, "Although love is primarily motivated by desire, it is deeply inclined toward affection and no living creature can escape from it." He states positively, "Fondness for sensual pleasures is common to all, regardless of time and space." He gives an explanation as to why monks write many love poems. Since monks "do not have wives and are always restrained from satisfying their desire, . . . it tends to lie embedded in their minds" and "they express it more sentimentally than worldly people would in love poems."[36] Although Norinaga divided love into two phases, desire and affection, he asserted the importance of physicality in love, for he felt that love is primarily motivated by desire.[37]

Yet there are many even how who think that seeing love as a composite of desire and affection is blending love with obscenity. Therefore, when a girl wants to marry another boy, giving her sweetheart the brush-off, if she says, "Even though I marry another boy, my heart is always yours," the sweetheart is apt to be obsessed

---

35. Shikitei Sanba, *Ukiyoburo* [Chattering Bathers in a Public Bathhouse] (1806–1813).

36. Motoori Norinaga, *Isonokami sasamegoto* [Whispered Words of the Past] (1763).
37. Ibid.

with the idea that he is the victor in love, in spite of the fact that he is actually losing her.

A man like Yamada Kōsaku, who does not appreciate such parting words, is therefore considered to be exceptional. When his lover was about to be married to another man, "I received a letter from her. It read: 'I love you! Even though I submit my flesh to another man, my soul is yours. . . .' To hell with you! That's how I felt. How does she make a distinction between the flesh and the soul?"[38] This is physicality in love, and it may sound sordid to many Japanese people. However, even Norinaga, who lived several hundred years ago, distinctly asserted that love has two phases, physical and spiritual, which seems like rather a sound philosophy of love.

Dazai Osamu in his humorous short story entitled *Chance* similarly makes fun of spiritualism in love and gives a physical definition of love: "Often an affected woman says, 'Let us cherish our affection without having a love affair. Would you please be my older brother?' . . . When she utters such words, she is giving me the brush-off. . . . To hell with 'love'! Be your older brother? Don't be a fool! Who would dare become your older brother? That's a different story! . . . Love is amorousness, culturally and newly rephrased, that is, desire between man and woman motivated by sexual impulse."[39]

Cheap magazines, stripteases, and prostitutes are the revelations of postwar physicality and are the phenomena of a transitional period; however, the fight for the sexual emancipation seen in the trials connected with *Lady Chatterley's Lover* marks a summit of physicality in Japan in terms of the logical assertion of sound physicality in love. It is evidence that a healthy physicality has begun to take root in the psychology of the Japanese people.

---

38. Yamada Kōsaku, "Shakkin no kotsu" ["How to Borrow Money"] *King* 29, no. 9 (1953).
39. Dazai Osamu, "Chansu" ["Chance"], *Geijutsu* 7 (1946).

6. Human Relationships

So far I have described the main characteristics of the psychology of the Japanese people. The bottom layer of the foundation on which that psychology rests is Japan's social structure, evolved over many centuries.

Japan's social structure is supposedly based on a capitalistic economy, but it retains remnants of feudalism, particularly in human relationships. Modern and traditional phases are intermingled: in Japan the delicate balance of new and old is their most outstanding characteristic.

Although human psychology is fundamentally regulated by the social structure, it is more directly a response to human relationships. Therefore, I would like to give a broad view of the various types of human relationships in present-day Japan to clarify what I have described so far.

The element that has not been modernized in human relationships in Japan is the link of feudalistic obligation called *giri*. The promise that controls human relationships in a capitalistic society is obligation backed by rights. In Japan, this modern obligation and feudalistic *giri* are delicately entangled and make human relationships very complicated. Let us examine how *giri* and the human relationships derived from it affect the social psychology of the Japanese.

Life Is Full of Giri

The word *giri* has various meanings. In the widest sense, the character *gi* signifies that each individual acts according to the understanding of how he should be. The word *giri* simply means the reason for *gi* (right-doing). Therefore, *giri* or *gi* is a promise to act in a fitting manner according to where one stands in relation to others in the social structure. And the promise, unlike modern obligation, is not grounded in rights. *Giri* is rather a promise of a certain attitude or conduct toward all of the people who surround one. When the promise is widely interpreted, it becomes *sekentei* (social reputation, appearance) or *giri* to society.

Although *giri* assumes varied forms depending on whether the relationship is between parent and child, man and wife, or a person and his relatives, friends, superiors, or inferiors, it demands, in any case, that a man accept the obligation as a long-established promise and act upon it as he should without asking for a logical explanation.

The character *gi*, therefore, was said to mean "resolution not discordant with reason even to the slightest degree; that is, man lives when he should live and dies when he should die."[1] In shingaku, *gi* connotes "doing nothing unreasonable and immoderate." It is proper that a servant be diligent in service and that a wife take good care of her husband. This propriety is taught as the way of man.[2]

In brief, *giri* implies that one is satisfied with one's lot in the existing society; it is a forced promise to rationalize the practice of no self, acquiring the spirit of service above self. *Giri* generally operates when a superior demands loyalty and service from his inferiors. Conversely, his *giri* to them causes him to show affection and gratitude in some form.

Take the words "favor of the lord," for instance. This favor is given in return for the loyalty and service of a warrior, and loyalty never did mean unilateral sacrifice. The word *on* (a debt of gratitude) was used in the past to describe a superior's gratitude for the services rendered by his inferiors. *Family Precepts of Ise Sadatake* reads: "A lord's *giri* is not to make a favor of furnishing stipends and allowances

---

1. Muro Naokiyo, *Gojō gorin meigi* [Justification of the Five Virtues and the Five Relations] (1723).
2. Kyūō, *Kyūō dōwa* [Kyūō's Moral Discourses] (1834).

but to be obliged to do so and to be delighted by his retainers' pains and services."[3] Both the high and the low were said to be obliged to one another.

Giri is not one-sided; neither is loyalty. The view that it would be better for a man to serve his lord according to the degree of the lord's favor is often observed in books on the way of the warrior. *Basic Principles of the Way of the Warrior* says that since there are two classes of servants in a warrior family and those below *ashigaru* (foot soldiers), such as *kobito* (errand men) and *chūgen* (manservants) are furnished with small stipends and allowances, they are not to be harshly judged if they flee or behave in a cowardly fashion when a battle is about to take place. On the contrary, those who have lain under a deep obligation for several generations or years and who are under the day to day favor of the lord must fight in return for this favor and affection without regard for their lives.[4]

The people lower on the scale, therefore, are not necessarily obliged to the lord, for day to day favor is scarcely given to them; they are not bound by mutual obligation.[5] One's sense of *giri* is deepened in exact proportion to the favor of a lord. Viewed from this angle, both loyalty and service among the warriors of the Tokugawa period implied, to a considerable degree, an exchange or a contract.

In the moral code designed for the retention of the emperor system after the Meiji period, only sacrificial service was emphasized. As seen in the first chapter, absolute submission to authority and denial of self were imposed upon the whole people, and loyalty, as *giri*, became one-sided. Let me quote examples from two books written during the war.

It was said that "every service must start out with sincerity, as if one were serving the Emperor"; "true selfless devotion" is "the way

3. Ise Sadatake, *Ise Sadatake kakun* [Family Precepts of Ise Sadatake] (1763).
4. Daidōji Yūzan, *Budō shoshinshū* [Basic Principles of the Way of the Warrior] (1834).
5. Ibid.

of a subject." It was even said that "apart from this life of service, there is no such thing as a private life."⁶ This is an absolutely slavish service, different from the loyalty of the historical *giri*.

Foot soldiers in the past could flee for their lives; however, under the fascist system dedicated to the Emperor, "no service is great enough"; "death in consequence of one's endless service is most worthy." In such a system service is not rendered in exchange for remuneration.⁷

To my surprise, even after the war, there exist ex-military officers who proclaim publicly that this attitude of service above self is the nature of the Japanese. One of the writers of *The Kamikaze Suicide Units*, in answer to questions from the U.S. Board of Inquiry, said, "To offer one's whole self to the Emperor [the word includes the concept of fatherland] is the essential nature or being of the Japanese. . . . I believe that the *kamikaze* suicide attacks resulted from this idea and were a direct manifestation of it."⁸

The loyalty of the people, of course, is spoken of in contrast to imperial favors, so that it does not look one-sided but seems to contain an exchange. In fact, if the people had not assumed that this exchange existed, they would have become disgusted with the situation.

In the past even a *daimyō* (feudal lord), Tachibana Muneshige, said that a lord should hold his retainers as dear as his own children. Otherwise, "when men, even if they belonged to my family, stood face to face with the enemy . . . they would not follow me, even if I simply commanded them to advance or die."⁹

There must have been many such soldiers who faced battle, re-

6. Sonda Hideharu, *Shinmin no michi kaisetsu taisei* [Complete Works for the Exposition of the Way of the Subject] (Tokyo: Taimeidō, 1942).

7. Ōkura Kunihiko, *Musubi no sangyō* [Industrial Activity Based on the Spirit of *Musubi*] (Tokyo: Dainihon Sangyō Hōkoku Kai, 1942).

8. Inokuchi Rikihei and Nakajima Tadashi, *Kamikaze tokubetsu kōgekitai* [The *Kamikaze* Suicide Units] (Tokyo: Nihon Shuppan Kyōdō Kabushiki Gaisha, 1951).

9. Tachibana Muneshige, *Tachibana ryūsai kakun okitesho* [Family Precepts of Tachibana Muneshige] (1628).

solving, "food and clothing have been generously bestowed on us soldiers at the front. Who would not repay this someday?"[10] Military men, in contrast with civilians, were blessed with food and clothing during the war.

Giri also exists between parent and child in the form of a child's filial devotion and filial piety given in return for his parent's love. In this instance, love between parent and child and *giri* are fused, and *giri* and *ninjō* (human feeling) are usually undifferentiable. However, a child is required to show special respect and submission to his father as the head of the family. At this point, the affection between parent and child seen outside Japan is supplemented by what a child should be according to *giri*.

In relationships between an individual and his father- or mother-in-law, especially between a mother-in-law and daughter-in-law, although nominally parent-child relationships, *giri* is predominant. As in the case of *samurai* loyalty, it "becomes grim in proportion to the amount of property. . . . The wealthier the family, the grimmer the mother-in-law, for she thinks that her daughter-in-law must give service worthy of the property."[11] In short, the expression of *giri* in service is different from filial piety toward one's real parents, which arises from *ninjō*.

The most conspicuous aspects of family relationships in Japan today, except for those in the fishing villages, are found in farming villages. Here the father as head of the family holds more power than the mother, despite the fact that both are parents, and the position of the oldest son is considerably higher than that of his brothers and sisters. This is the very basis of the predominance of man over woman still rooted in the Japanese people. As a result, it is natural that such phrases as "as a man," "like a man," "a man-to-man talk," "display one's manliness," and "a man's word" ring out in the Diet.

---

10. Yoshida Mitsuru, *Senkan Yamato no saigo* [The Final Day of the Batteship *Yamato*] (Tokyo: Sōgensha, 1952).

11. Ōmura Ryō, "Nōson no sekentei" ["The Public Appearance of the Farming Village"], *Tōyō Bunka* 12 (1953).

As a father and his oldest son form a sort of union of authority, a mother and her daughters are prone to form a spiritual counterteam against the men. Therefore, many girls in Japan seem today to have a sense of *giri* to their mothers rather than to their fathers. Many examples of reminiscences describing *giri* to one's mother are found in the confessions made by prostitutes and delinquent girls: "From now on, I would like to bear any hardship, work earnestly to turn over a new leaf, and show my serious self to my deceased mother." "I would like to straighten out, go home, beg my mother's forgiveness, and work earnestly. Please let me stay with my mother."[12]

However, the important role played in society by family relationships in Japan is not confined to individual families. The fact is that a similar pattern has spread to every human relationship in Japan. It has been said that since the Japanese family stresses parent and child relationships and is centered on the head of the family, unlike the unit focused upon a couple found abroad, it is natural for people to have a regard for filial piety.[13]

Giri in this parent and child relationship, since the father as head of the family presides over the whole family with competence and initiative and does not differ from a superior officer in the army,[14] elicits behavior which makes the family the basic unit and fashions all other social groups after it. These human relationships based on familism are uniquely Japanese.

This relationship of boss (parent status) and follower (child status) has adults of Japan playing the role of parent or child not only in the family but also in social groups. Since a majority of the Japanese are compelled to play the role of father or child in social groups other than the family, a tendency for domestic fussiness and indulgence becomes part of the psychology of the Japanese. A paternalism unique to human relationships is the result of this tendency. That is, a superior

---

12. Takenaka Katsuo, *Gaishō* [Streetgirls—Actual Conditions and Their Memoirs] (Tokyo: Yūkōsha, 1949).
13. Sonda, *Way of the Subject.*
14. Ōkura, *Industrial Activity.*

not only treats his inferiors with parental love, seeing them as his children and caring for them, but he also looks down upon them as mere children and is aware that he is supposed to love those around him from a step higher, train them, and initiate them.[15]

One's paternalism therefore, is often accompanied by a posture of looking down upon one's inferiors and despising them. Although the person concerned may not be conscious of it, this attitude is like the authority of the head of a family in the sense that he is, candidly speaking, looking down from a step higher.

Obviously, this paternalism was adopted by the military who took the family sentiment of the Japanese and put it into a more distinct form. The following song reveals this atmosphere well: "The company commander says, in an instruction, 'I'm your father, the squad leaders are your mothers, and the senior comrades are your big brothers. I hope you will all get along with one another, be in good health, and serve out your time safely.' Tear-jerking, indeed, is the instruction; it turns into a demon when a night passes."[16] The tone of this song is really pitiful: soldiers of Japan were treated like children in a family and, like stepchildren, were given a demon's chastisement when a night passed. An ex-officer explained this familism: "A warrant officer . . . plays a subordinate role in that he takes care of soldiers like their mother. . . . A company commander is strict like a father on the one hand. On the other hand, he treats soldiers with the love given his own flesh and blood, so to speak, and brings his orders home to their minds."[17]

The ideal of the military must have been to build up human relationships like the one shown in the following episode, to have soldiers feel about their officer as if he were a reliable father. "On November 30, 1905, I participated in the battle of 203-Meter Hill as a

---

15. Ibid.

16. Noma Hiroshi, *Shinkū chitai* [The Vacuum Zone] (Tokyo: Kawade Shobō, 1952).

17. Iizuka Kōji, *Nihon no guntai* [The Japanese Military] (Tokyo: Tokyo Daigaku Shuppanbu, 1950).

company commander. . . . The battle took place on a dark night and the commander was not visible; the soldiers must have felt helpless. I sometimes heard a shout, 'Where is the officer?' When I answered, saying, 'Here I am,' they must have felt relieved because I again heard their vigorous war cries. At first, someone else also gave a reply; later I was the only one who responded."[18]

Such a sense of trust is built up only in a relationship similar to that of parent and child. This illustrates an important phase of the Japanese psychology, for the Japanese try to lean on the family relationship even after they grow up. This is what prevents the ego from developing. In other words, the adults of Japan retain a mentality that is childish in many respects.

On the other hand, the paternalism of Japan's leaders develops an abnormal psychology: they do not mind sacrificing their subordinates although they are as dear to them as their children. Lieutenant Colonel Tamai, commander of the *kamikaze* suicide units, addressed his subordinates: "I always regard you with deep affection, as a parent cares for his children, often thinking, 'what dears they are.' I have always thought of you and tried to find a good opportunity for you to make yourselves useful."[19] Taking the consequences into consideration, such paternal love was, indeed, an unwelcome favor to Japan's youth.

Besides such distinct vertical relationships as those between lord and retainer or parent and child, *giri* lingers on in relations between merchant and customer: a merchant treats his customers almost as if they were his masters. In one of the most modern department stores in Tokyo, "customers have long been called *zenshu*. . . . This means 'master' and is an honorific name for 'customer'." Employees are always instructed, "The new democracy should not be reflected in your attitude toward customers."[20]

---

18. Uchiyama Yūjiro, *Senjō shinrigaku* [Battlefield Psychology] (Tokyo: Kaikōsha, 1930).
19. Inokuchi and Nakajima, *Suicide Units*.
20. "Pyramid," department store bulletin.

Giri is still highly regarded, at least among older people, as a social promise. This is clearly observable in *A Survey of Public Opinion on Social Education* (*Shakai kyōiku ni tsuite no yoron chōsa*, March 1953) made by the National Public Opinion Research Institute. "There are people who deplore that many in these regrettable times do not know what *giri* is. Do you feel the same?" In answer to the question, about 70 percent of the replies of people in all age groups were "I feel sad too." Needless to say, since this is a leading question and the connotation of *giri* varies considerably with the respondents, this percentage should not be accepted at face value. Yet there still remain expressions such as "Japan's special product are *giri* and *ninjō*," which seems to show that a sense of *giri* is deeply rooted in the minds of the Japanese.

When *giri* is applied not just to limited individuals such as superiors or the head of a family but to the whole society, it becomes regard for one's name or social reputation. "Society" here refers neither to the group which knows one through wide social reputation nor to the public which forms a judgment. It is rather the individual's personal milieu, which varies with the individual.

To some people, "society" means only their neighborhood. Political leaders may take it in terms of Japan as a whole. Therefore, in the narrowest sense, *giri* to society involves not making a bad show for the sake of the neighborhood. What one's association with one's neighbors should be is determined by *giri*. *Giri* to the whole society is a promise not to ruin one's name, not to lose face before society.

The word *seken-sama*, "society," connotes a feeling of appreciation for the benefits betowed by the society. In other words, since a man has favors bestowed on him in some form by society, he serves society by abiding by his *giri* to society because, "I am indebted for my chance to make a living to my country, my ancestors, and my surroundings."[21] The word "surroundings" means "society" here.

The Japanese people, therefore, are rendering a kind of service to

---

21. Ōkura, *Industrial Activity*.

society by incessantly abiding by *giri*. In the public opinion research cited earlier, in reply to the question, "What kind of person does not have a sense of *giri?*" 30 percent of the respondents said, "One who does not know what a debt of gratitude is"; 10 percent of them answered, "An egoist"; and many said repayment of a favor or service was demanded by *giri*.

Work for Riches Rather than Giri

Giri, a promise in a feudalistic and old-fashioned human relationship, and conduct motivated by gain in contrast to *gi* (right-doing) have long been said to conflict. In *Precepts for the Warrior*, for instance, it says: "A warrior should be especially aware of *giri*. He who is sharply conscious of *giri* is inattentive to gain." The love of gain of the townsman was thus mentioned in contrast to the *giri* of the warrior; however, love of gain was never seen as an immoral desire for townsmen. On the contrary, Nishikawa Joken flatly rejected fame, a kind of *giri*, saying, "When a townsman seeks after fame, disregarding gain, he will surely lose his property."[22] In *shingaku* too, as Baigan said, "A merchant's getting profit is as good as a warrior's receiving a stipend";[23] gaining profit was taken as a matter of course for a townsman.

There even existed the idea that since love of gain, for townsmen, always took precedence over *giri*, there was for them no such *giri* as loyalty or service. Nishikawa Joken positively stated: "A townsman has no masters. He has only parents. The most unfilial conduct is to take part in warriorlike action. . . . A townsman must be thankful for being born a townsman."[24] He goes on to tell this story. A townsman was told by a monk, "Since you have a good attitude of mind, you may be reborn a warrior in the next life." He answered,

---

22. Nishikawa Joken, *Chōnin bukuro* [Lot of the Townsman] (1719).
23. Baigan, *Tohi mondō* [Moral Lesson of Shingaku] (1739).
24. Nishikawa, *Lot of the Townsman*.

"That's a pretty annoyance, to be born a warrior! I would like to enjoy the life of a townsman rather than to serve under a lord, fearing him, having no time to set my mind at rest, endeavoring to attain fame with the sole aim of astounding my fellow warriors, and appreciating the pleasure of a stiff manner."[25]

To persist in *giri* and neglect gain is seen as ridiculous in the present morality of tradesmen. *Tōkyū-jutsu* also encourages them to seek gain rather than *gi*. "There is a proverb 'Work for riches rather than *giri*; earn money rather than stubbornly pursuing a trifle.' You should not be obstinate but keep pace with the times. It is more profitable to work for riches than *giri*."[26]

A Dilemma between Giri and Ninjo

The more common form of resistance to *giri* is a demand for humanity expressed in the word *ninjō* (human feeling). *Giri* and *ninjō* have customarily been used together; however, *ninjō* is, in fact, limited by the promise of *giri*. Therefore, a confrontation or a dilemma between *giri* and *ninjō* has cast a unique shadow on the Japanese mind.

This dilemma is most tormenting to the Japanese. Thus, a work which delineates the pitiful situation of someone bearing downheartedness patiently because he has no solution to it arouses sympathy in Japanese readers. This sympathy is very different from the sympathy aroused by foreign dramas in which tragedy is a result of a character flaw. Unlike the foreign tragedies in which failure or decline appeals to readers and spectators, Japanese tragedies focus on an unsolved or stagnant situation.

Let me use an example from a *rōkyoku* chant. The mother of a

---

25. Ibid.
26. Yōshin-dō and Shōyō-do, *Tōkyu-jutsu kōwa* [A System of Astrology] (Tokyo: Eirakudo, 1912).

yakuza, for respectability's sake, holds back her eagerness to see her son who has come home. "While listening to her son's voice, the mother, screened from his sight by shutters, yearns for him. She refrains from embracing him because of the rule of the floating world. She burns for him like the silent firefly and does not cry out like the cicada." Bearing her emotion patiently, she forbears from crying and follows, at least formally, the rule of the floating world, *giri*. And the more suppressed by *giri* the outlet for *ninjō* is, the more purified, deepened, and intensified *ninjō* becomes. This is the balance between *giri* and *ninjō*.

This way of looking at life, as a dilemma between *giri* and *ninjō*, is clearly revealed in the *rōkyoku* chant "A *Yakusa* Story" by Chichibu Shigetake. "Knowing how bitter the floating world is, we tend to become sentimental. The human mind is weak, so we live together, helping one another, and here *giri* and *ninjō* bloom."

Eulogizing the human situation in a dilemma is not limited to the old-fashioned *rōkyoku* chants. Forbearing in a dilemma between love and society arouses deep sympathy even in modern audiences, and many popular songs deal with this type of situation. "If true love is to endure tears and give up the name of mother, let me just sing a lullaby, embracing the image of my dear child." ("Mother in the Moonlight") "A wind whispers to me that you have already been a wife at a hot spring. Ah, let the feelings that I can no longer express openly, even if I were to meet you, be conveyed in a song and arouse an echo in your heart!" ("Elegy in a Hot Springs Town")

Japanese movies called *haha-mono* (mother films) and *namida-mono* (tear films) have as their theme the sorrow of a mother who cannot introduce herself to her child. From prewar times to the present, tragedies depicting a dilemma between *giri* and maternal love have been produced repeatedly, all with a similar plot; they move female fans to tears and are box-office successes. *Haha-mono* and *namida-mono* are barometers that indicate how frequently similar dilemmas occur in human relationships in Japan.

Don't Take Giri and Ninjo Seriously

In opposition to this entanglement of *giri* and *ninjō*, a naturalism based on the denial of *giri* and *ninjō* has arisen. It attempts to free man's simple desires from the frame of *giri* and advocates rationalism in life in an attempt to create new human relationships in place of *giri* and *ninjō*.

Naturalism which denies *giri* is related to physicality which values the desires of the body. Arguments that stand on physicality and deny Japan's feudalistic human relationships are emphasized in *On Corruption* by Sakaguchi Ango and *A Courageous Freedom* by Matsunaga Yasuzaemon, both of which I have frequently cited. Sakaguchi wrote, "To remove such hypocritical trappings as the prohibition of adultery or *giri* and *ninjō* is the first condition to restore humanity."[27] Matsunaga said, "Such sentiments as feudalistic *giri* and *ninjō* are nonsense when viewed beside true human affection."[28] These utterances are still new: such denials of *giri* and *ninjō* are often mistaken as immoderate egoism aimed at allowing licentiousness.

An attempt to make human relationships in Japan reasonable and suited to the modern world has to start with a readjustment of the overburdensome *giri* and *ninjō*. Rationalism in life should be useful for this purpose, if properly directed. But rationalism, I regret to say, tends to go to excess and to fall into schemes motivated by egoism unmindful of annoying others.

Therefore, even when a politician named Hirokawa Kōzen advanced the following argument against *giri* and *ninjō*, he appears not to be speaking in favor of rationalistic politics so much as to be excusing his own lack of *giri* and *ninjō* toward his boss, Yoshida Shi-

---

27. Sakaguchi Ango, "Daraku ron" ["On Corruption"], *Shinchō* 43, no. 4 (1946).
28. Matsunaga Yasuzaemon, *Yūki aru jiyū* [A Courageous Freedom] (Tokyo: Kaname Shobō, 1953).

geru. "Generally speaking, policy and *giri* and *ninjō* should be distinctly distinguished in politics. Therein lies the value of politics. If everything, even a wrong, were to be regulated by *giri* and *ninjō*, what consequences there would be in politics. If the boss were to commit a wrong and cause a scandal and all of us were to follow him because of *giri* and *ninjō*, what consequences there would be."[29]

Ichikawa Fusae says that Hirokawa's rationalism, "is a kind of advancement. I believe it is good that political *giri* and *ninjō* should die out."[30] However, in Japan, it is hard to discuss rationalism generally unless you specify whose rationalism you are considering. As Abe Shinnosuke said at the same discussion meeting, "It is feudalistic to harshly criticize someone who has betrayed his master."[31] Hirokawa's words in that respect speak of a rationalization of politics.

An excessive form of rationalism that denies *giri* and *ninjō* and has made itself most conspicuous after the war is the contractualism thought out by Yamazaki of the Hikari Club, who attempted to rationalize every human relationship in terms of a contract. He developed contractualism out of his unique brand of rationalism discussed earlier.

According to him, since "relations between man and man . . . are rationalized according to the basic principle of international law, 'mutual consent shall be binding,' . . . it is not necessary to abide by any rules set by man other than that."[32] *Giri* and *ninjō* are out of the question.

This applies to romance too. "You should never go against what you have contracted. In other words, if you say to a man, 'I love you,' and look at another man thirty minutes later, that is wrong.

---

29. Hirokawa Kōzen, "Rakusen no ben" ["An Excuse for Defeat in the Election— No Self-Criticism Is Necessary"], *Bungei Shunjū* 31, no. 8 (1953).

30. Ichikawa Fusae, "Nihon meibutsu giri ninjō" ["*Giri* and *Ninjō*, the Special Japanese Products"], *Bungei Shunjū* 31, no. 7 (1953).

31. Ibid.

32. Yamazaki Akitsugu, *Watakushi wa giakusha* [I Pretend to Be Evil] (Tokyo: Seinen Shobō, 1950).

You are carrying out an illegal act." Of marriage he said, "You should agree mutually that either of you can get a divorce from the other . . . make a marriage contract into a notarial deed."[33]

To Yamazaki, the relationship between parent and child is also a relationship by contract: "Why should you listen to your parents? . . . Because they feed you. In other words, you should be obedient in return for salary."[34]

Since contractualism permeates American society, the parent and child relationship proposed by Yamazaki might not particularly arouse a negative feeling in American readers. However, to the Japanese it sounds heartless owing to the prominence of *giri* and *ninjō*.

Inasmuch as parents in America set a consideration and negotiate with their children prior to sending them on an errand or having them do house repairs, their relations seem to rest upon something like a contract. Such a relationship appears, to the Japanese people, to trample *giri* and *ninjō* between parent and child. Since *giri* and *ninjō* linger on, when one becomes antagonistic to them, there is apt to be an excessive reaction, such as contractualism.

> Then the pale colonel and I were at last engaged. That was really unusual. We exchanged written contracts. We sealed them with our thumbmarks. But I, in fact, was not thinking of marriage that seriously. Therefore, the colonel was the buyer and I was the seller. The article for sale and the seller were one and the same, and the article was as good as new. Fulfillment of the promise would be in 1954, two years hence. We arranged it and made a contract quite lightly.[35]

This is a part of the notes left behind by a young woman, Kusaka Yōko, a nominee for the Akutagawa Prize who committed suicide after the war. Although the contract seems to have been exchanged

---

33. Ibid.
34. Ibid.
35. Kusaka Yōko, "Ikudome kano saiki" ["Many a Last Moment"], *Shinchō* 50, no. 5 (1953).

half in fun, it reveals the philosophy of contractualism more or less common to the young postwar generation.

Both Yamazaki and Kusaka Yōko must have attempted, because of youth's distrust of man, to control their human relationships by believing in and fulfilling contracts that bind men in some form. Yamazaki, when he was unable to cover his debts, applied the principle of unavoidable alteration by circumstance. Since "a contract . . . is not applicable to that matter called a corpse, . . . I observe my logical consistency by reducing myself to matter"; he killed himself, thus fulfilling his contractualism.[36] Being troubled over a love triangle, being perplexed in a dilemma between art and life, and breaking the written marriage contract, Kusaka took her own life. The end of contractualism in both cases was death. This was because they not only opposed the old-fashioned *giri* and *ninjō* but also denied human love and trust.

In comparison to these two, those who from prewar times have been persistent in the belief that they are not wedded to *giri* and *ninjō* look upon contractualism in a sunnier form. The view on love contracts held by Yamada Kōsaku, whom I have previously cited as an advocate of physicality, is an example: "A man falls in one-sided love with a woman. When she marries another man, he calls it his disappointment in love. It is not truly disappointment in love because no contract was ever made."[37]

The Japanese are not accustomed to the word "contractualism." However, when the rationalization of living is taken into consideration, contractualism, like physicality, is an unavoidable road which they must walk at least once, even if they follow it too far.

---

36. Yamazaki, *I Pretend to Be Evil.*
37. Yamada Kōsaku, "Shakkin no kotsu" ["How to Borrow Money"] *King* 29, no. 9 (1953).

Distinguish between Your Public Self and
Your Private Self

If *giri* is a promise in personal and social relationships, *honbun* (primary duty) is broader in meaning. It indicates one's place in society and the pattern of conduct befitting that place. Words such as *bun, bunzai,* and *bungen* corresponding to types of *honbun* have been used traditionally. *Honbun* in relation to one's profession is called *shokubun* (professional status and duty), whereas *honbun* in the social classification system is called *mibun* (social status).

Honbun is a vestige of the *bungen* and *bunzai* human relationships of the feudal society, and those old elements are intermingled in the human relationships of contemporary Japanese society. The *honbun* of today, unlike the *bungen* of the past, is not dependent on one's social status or trade acquired at birth. In that respect, *honbun* is a human relationship in which one can select one's own position to a certain extent.

However, *honbun,* like *bungen,* binds man's life for twenty-four hours a day. This is one of the ways it differs from ordinary service. In other words, the *honbun* of an employee of a company and the *honbun* of a student at school can restrain them even outside office or school hours. They are restricted by their *honbun* not only in terms of time but of space: employees are required to abide by and act upon the employee's *honbun* outside of the company, as are students.

The "Summary of the Employee's Duties" of the Tokyo department store mentioned earlier, for example, admonishes employees that "since the public looks upon your speech and behavior as that of an employee of the store even outside working hours, be attentive to your speech and behavior in your private life and never compromise your honor as an employee of the store."

If circumstances are such in a private enterprise, it is not difficult to imagine how much more prevalent this attitude is in public offices. In the past there was the Public Service Personnel Code, and today in the Public Service Law and other regulations, the *honbun* of public service personnel is subject to very minute legal restrictions, such as the restriction of political activity while off duty.

In other words, for the majority of Japanese, the so-called "public hours," work, encroach upon their private lives, and in the most extreme cases, public life eats up private life. The public life of a company employee compels him, even after office hours, to attend midnight banquets and deprives him of almost all the hours of his private life. This kind of obligation is so irrational that foreigners are never able to understand it. At the same time, this overflow of public into private life is one of the major causes of the lack of distinction between public and private individuals or public and private affairs in Japan.

The Japanese do not mix public and private matters only on account of self-interest and avarice. Inasmuch as public and private matters are jumbled up in *honbun*, it may be unreasonable to tell people to differentiate between public affairs and private ones. Bribery, corruption, favoritism, and a system of perquisites are inevitable, for in the social life of the Japanese, public and private life are confused. *Honbun* is clamorously emphasized all over the country, yet the more public life encroaches upon private life, the more behavior which is unfitting to *honbun* increases. This vicious circle is inevitable and cannot be stopped in the present social structure of Japan.

When the originally feudalistic *honbun* relationship is brought into a modern society grounded upon a capitalistic economy, one can do whatever wrong one thinks fit when one mixes *honbun* with self-interest and avarice. It is no wonder that the book on the art of living quoted earlier even teaches one how to take bribe.

Everyone Tries to Escape from Duty

In any profession in modern society, whatever it may be, one is entrusted with authority in proportion to one's position but one also has to assume responsibility. In Japanese society officials are a good example of this. The balance between authority and responsibility in *honbun* is weighted on one side; it is characterized by a large proportion of authority. Imai Kazuo, an official, talks honestly about this point. He says that in Japan's public offices "there are quite minute regulations concerning authority, yet there is scarcely a regulation as to how far one has to assume responsibility when one fails in an assigned task."[38]

The balance between authority and responsibility was one-sided in military life as well as in official life. For example, up until the defeat, petty officers could "use sailors as we pleased and exercise the greatest authority in a position of no responsibility. This was the pleasure of navy life."[39]

Furthermore, the authority of Japanese officials is not confined to dutiful performance of assignments: the so-called perquisites come in train. Perquisites are not an officially recognized consideration such as prerogatives and privileges but are unofficially accepted in public offices through tacit understanding. A large part of the public knows about these perquisites and complains but thinks they are legal.

Indeed, perquisites are a direct result of the confusion of public and private life, so that official authority is carried into unofficial life. This, too, flows from the view that *honbun* binds a man's life twenty-four hours a day. When a policeman is given preferential treatment at a restaurant, he is being given *kowamote* (treatment motivated by fear); he avails himself of the *honbun* of a policeman, and

---

38. Imai Kazuo, *Kanryō* [Bureaucrat] (Tokyo: Yomiuri Shimbun, 1953).
39. Iizuka, *Japanese Military*.

citizens who know what he is doing don't have the courage to protest. Rather, the restaurant owner welcomes such perquisites for the sake of business because he, in exchange, gets favors from the police.

In the *honbun* relationship, authority is endlessly expanded in the form of perquisites, but responsibility, on the other hand, is avoided as much as possible. It is not an overstatement to say that the ability of an official is synonymous with his ability to shirk responsibility. A superior evades responsibility, saying, "I've left the matter to my subordinate," or "Such a matter is handled by the office." A subordinate avoids responsibility, saying, "I've been waiting for my superior's decision," or "Since I'm an office clerk, I cannot give you any responsible answer." The political ability of an official is judged by his skillfulness or lack thereof in this type of maneuvering. Officials are supposed to be public servants, yet they adopt a course of action in which, with political ability, they repeat excuses and ambiguous answers until the general citizen gives up.

An evasion of responsibility can be achieved in two ways: making an official's responsibility as small as possible and keeping the knowledge of the actual locus of responsibility from the citizens. Every public officeholder, whether in vertical or horizontal relationships, tries to be a good boy by shifting the responsibility to others when something goes wrong.

From one point of view this evasion of responsibility not only indicates shrewdness and selfishness but reveals the lack of self-confidence and the weakness of character prevalent among the Japanese. The emphasis of the phrases "cut your coat according to your cloth" or "demote yourself from your station in life"[40] has succeeded in making people timid, always careful to be unassuming, taking no responsibility, reserved. In this respect, the evasion of responsibility might be considered a product of the peculiar psychology created by Japan's feudalistic human relationships.

This evasion of responsibility, therefore is often observable not

---

40. Izawa Nagahide, *Bushikun* [Precepts for the Warrior] (1715).

only among officials but also among private citizens. As is often pointed out by foreigners, this tendency is clearly shown in the fact that the Japanese do not directly negotiate a matter of importance between the persons concerned but have a go-between to take care of the negotiation. There are some foreigners who interpret this tendency favorably: the Japanese are conscious of not impairing the other party's honor and as a result do things through a third person. However, the element of evasion of responsibility seems quite prominent.

Conclusion

As we have observed, *giri* and *ninjō* govern human relationships in Japan and prevent people from negotiating face-to-face as individuals. *Giri* and *ninjō* create vagueness between individuals. Everyone wears a kind of kimono called *honbun* (primary duty) and lives without showing his plain self; everyone is surrounded by an air of uncertainty.

The "something that cannot be rationalized" and "something above reason" common to the irrationalism, spiritualism, and imperfectionism of the Japanese that I have described in this book seem to be created out of the uncertainties hanging over these human relationships.

Foreigners criticize the Japanese because what they are thinking is imperceptible, because they are unfathomable. This criticism results from a superficial view; their understanding of these particular human relationships is shallow.

In order to create a new Japan, we must endeavor to reconstruct its social foundation and wipe away the vestiges of the past, the ambiguous human relationships and the blurs in social psychology originating from them. It is difficult for each individual to anticipate happiness unless the reconstruction of society makes headway, keeping pace with the reconstruction of man.

This book may seem to have been devoted only to picking out flaws in the Japanese psychology. However, if we neglect to face our true selves, it will take more time to reconstruct our society. Unpleasant things are best cleared up at once. I have written this book in the hope that it will be helpful to some degree in accomplishing this task.